Late Bloomer

Late Bloomer

Profiles of women who found their true calling

Lois Rich-McCoy

HARPER & ROW, PUBLISHERS, New York
Cambridge, Hagerstown, Philadelphia, San Francisco,
London, Mexico City, São Paulo, Sydney

1817

"You are brilliant, beautiful, and able," she told me from the time I was a little girl, "and you can do whatever you want, whenever you wish."

Late Bloomer is dedicated to her.

For my mother, Ruth Rich

FIRST EDITION

Designer: Janice Stern

Library of Congress Cataloging in Publication Data

Rich-McCoy, Lois.
    Late bloomer.

    1. Middle aged women—United States—Biography.
    2. Women executives—United States—Biography.
    3. Self-employed—United States—Biography.
    I. Title.
    HQ1064.U5R52   301.41'2'0922   79-1679
    ISBN 0-06-013593-X

80 81 82 83 84 10 9 8 7 6 5 4 3 2 1

Contents

Introduction

Are you ready for a profession, capable of success? Have you been marking time during the first phase of your adulthood? Accumulating momentum? Has the gift of time, which men traditionally do not possess—they must make career decisions early on—allowed you to recognize your various abilities at last? And do you now need not philosophy but practical methodology and role models?

To bloom late, to realize one's potential, to turn one's life around, to start again—women in particular, flexible, innovative, adaptable women, are intrigued with the notion. They want to hear of people who did it, and how.

A special kind of woman—the Late Bloomer—turns her mature years into a personal springtime. After decades as an unfulfilled single woman or as a homemaker and raiser of children, she courageously decides to try something totally different and develops a new life and style within a responsible career.

As family responsibilities are satisfied, as inner motivation finally takes hold, perhaps after a husband dies or a divorce occurs, the Late Bloomer becomes a self-created success. From her rich life experiences, an idea emerges and takes more definite shape, a contemporary concept. She finds that what she has learned as a young full-time mother is applicable to the empty-nest years and to a second satisfying occupation. Women who chose to stay at home and raise their children needn't defend themselves, nor should they feel their usefulness has ended when their children are grown. For they have a chance to prove themselves worthwhile in the marketplace as well. And for the single or childless woman, the same opportunity exists for change.

I spoke of success as I toured the country in connection with my book *Millionairess: Self-Made Women of America,* about living females who did not inherit wealth and were personally and financially successful. And women in Atlanta, Houston, St. Paul, Boston consistently asked me, in hopeful voices, "Excuse me, but were any of these millionairesses late bloomers?" This expressed need for role models prompted my creation of *Late Bloomer*, not a philosophical treatise but a book about life, which speaks of fifteen women who, in their thirties, forties, fifties, and sixties, and with different family and educational backgrounds, began anew.

Late Bloomers—married, single, widowed, divorced—are special human beings. I respect these secure women who never seem at a disadvantage in any situation because, knowing their personal worth, they have built an inner esteem, a source of happiness.

After knowing them, I wondered, Is a female's late-occurring success sweeter than her male counterpart's? For she often has the advantage of choosing a vocation out of interest and desire, while financially supported by her husband.

There are numerous advantages in being female and wishing a delayed profession. And rather than lamenting problems, difficulties, the prospective Late Bloomer must, as do the fifteen profiled, take heed of the positive aspects of her situation.

The woman, often uniquely in a position to become a belated careerist, comes from a variety of circumstances.

The job of raising the family is completed. It is time to do something with the rest of her life.

She is newly widowed and, with her offspring grown, this empty-nester is lonely.

A victim of the Dumping Syndrome—her husband recently left her for the golden girl in the office—the divorcee belatedly recognizes the importance of having her own career: she must earn money to survive.

A single woman wants change. She sees new career opportunities she was unaware of, or which previously had not been available to her.

Again confronted at a party with, "I'm pleased to meet you. What does your husband do?" she realizes she wants to be able to give a new answer, involving her own accomplishments.

She needs to be more, or better, or different. It is time for growth.

Her children now attend grammar school. She would like to begin a career, perhaps on a part-time basis.

Everyone who knows her seems to agree that this middle-aged woman has the right to work, but she wonders about the risks. She worries about her husband's reaction.

Such women speak on these pages, heroically, with humor, and always positively, of their lives. From throughout the country, in a variety of fields, they gave their time, hospitality, and friendship and now allow us entry into their private and professional worlds. For you, the reader, I thank them.

You'll find a bit of yourself in each of the biographical profiles. Interviews with their husbands, friends, employees, parents, and children, as well as the Late Bloomers' own words, tell their stories and explore their childhoods, marriages, self-images, and attitudes toward the feminist movement—the whole range of pressures and problems, including a look at their families' often ambivalent reactions, is pondered.

The "How She Did It" listing at the end of each vignette offers clues to enable you, too, to blossom. And at the end of the biographies, we'll take a combined look at these achievers, with a quiz to help you evaluate yourself as a prospective Late Bloomer. By then, you'll realize that the question is not whether your ship will come in, but rather "Did I send one out?"

1

Leapfrog LaRouche

It is early evening in a rather depersonalized Central Park West apartment, an elegant Manhattan avenue but far enough uptown to be somewhat unfashionable. For the last ten minutes, the doorbell has been ringing spasmodically. Women trickle in past the dining room table covered with feminist pamphlets and articles, take seats in the semicircle of chairs in the living room, and immediately begin chatting. A fairly intimate knowledge of each other's lives is obvious. In spite of their interest in one another, the women seem impatient to begin. Frequent glances are directed toward the group's leader.

Janice LaRouche—a thin-boned, disheveled-looking woman, braless, wearing a paint-splattered shirt, with streaked gray-looking hair, no lipstick or jewelry—leans over her tape recorder and makes an adjustment. Sitting down, she crosses her dungaree-clad legs as she places a legal pad, covered with doodling, on her lap. Her pale face turns to the assembled group.

"Who would like to start?" she asks in her rather nasal New York voice. One is surprised at her enthusiasm; her expression suggested lethargy. A false impression.

The response to LaRouche's announcement that the counseling session has begun is immediate.

A twenty-two-year-old participant, in a three-piece navy suit and matching pumps, starts in a shaky voice: "I'd like to report modest progress. . . ."

D.A. hairdo of the fifties, Peter Pan collar, sitting primly: "We've got a new manager and things seem better. . . ."

Tall, stately full-length-corduroy-skirted: "I'd like to throw out a problem. . . ."

Shy, quiet voice, with a waist-long braid: "I'm entering into a very confused situation. . . ."

Gray flannel dress with matching short hair: "I'm thinking of quitting. . . ."

Perched on their chairs, they listen to their fellow counselees while keeping an eye on Ms. LaRouche, who is alert and interested, no matter how tedious the lamentation. There's a concerned feeling within the room; all seem to be involved with one another's problems. Some take notes.

As a participant presents a specific dilemma, LaRouche, whom *Forbes* calls "one of the most successful career counselors in the country," smiles and hits the root of the problem: "As usual, it's an abstract thought: 'How can I make these choices?' . . ." Then she initiates a discussion on the ability to take risks, which unfolds into a general discourse on job hunting, directed toward the group and at the same time answering the member's question.

Fifty-four-year-old LaRouche is clearly controlling the group's direction. Although the women will comment on each others' dilemmas, the career counselor analyzes and sums up. With a concerned expression, she asks brilliant rhetorical questions: When a woman complains that a co-worker was promoted above her, LaRouche realistically redirects the discussion toward reactions and recouping maneuvers. She admonishes in her slow voice: "You're not following a strategy; you're letting your anger control you," then explains the meaning of dignity and importance of professionalism.

There is no time at this meeting, it seems, for philosophizing and feminist theorizing. The problems are real and these ambitious working women look to LaRouche's career counseling service as an aid to climbing up their ladder more efficiently. How to be assertive yet nonaggressive. When to juggle priorities.

Ways to assure one is neither the squirmer nor the squirmee.

The group's interests and approaches are diverse. One woman likes to analyze the dynamics of a dialogue, another wants to switch careers but is unsure if she'll like her tentative choice. To her Janice responds: "Find out what someone's day is like." This woman nods, then jots a note to herself.

Janice manages the serious problems with a sense of humor; there is laughter at these meetings. "You sound like a different person than you were two weeks ago," LaRouche encourages one, then counsels: "Don't be moved around. Come up with a plan so you can be in charge," and to another, "Understand your *boss's* needs and goals." The woman bobs in agreement. The solutions seem so obvious when LaRouche presents them.

In fact a great deal of the LaRouche philosophy does appear to be self-evident, yet apparently there is a need for someone to expound it. Janice speaks of men picking up this kind of information—"a sense of the workplace"—throughout their development whereas females do not. She says women don't even know the language, for they've tuned it out since childhood. They absorbed homemaker-mother talk instead. And she laments that females, so brilliant in some ways, are totally naïve in these areas and are overpowered with their lack of knowledge and their weaknesses in the business world. "And I have to remind them, as a counselor, of their strengths. They don't see them, and they're often confronted with personnel interviewers who remind them, 'But you don't have this, but you don't know that.'"

LaRouche, who wove her way through these barriers herself, says that for a woman "to become a clerk-typist when she was a 'Mrs. Dr. Somebody' is extremely difficult. And to come from utilizing high-level organizing and coordinating skills in child rearing, homemaking—to have to go to the most basic, beginning baby steps of a career," is demeaning and difficult. "Work that's appropriate at age twenty is now handed to a forty-year-old mature woman. She must agree to accept low pay for a long time until she works her way up. These are not easy problems to cope with." LaRouche punctuates these disappointing and frustrating facts with, "Do it—by all means! *Go to it!*" As she did.

Janice LaRouche built a career as a counselor and formed career development workshops that *Forbes* referred to as "a kind of modern Dale Carnegie program for women." Yet successful, professional LaRouche—who spends her time teaching women how to jump into men's jobs—grew up within a family situation that she feels should have led inevitably to the traditional woman's role of mother and homemaker.

One of four children in a "very conventional" Jewish family, she was born in Far Rockaway on Long Island. Her father, a dress manufacturer, and her mother, who LaRouche feels was frustrated as a housewife, considered Janice's older sister to be the most intelligent and confident of the children. This sister, now married with three children, is, according to Janice, "a pro" as a homemaker. Janice's other sister is also a wife and mother. Her younger brother is a bookkeeper/accountant.

"I'm the only one who is an achiever, in the public view," states LaRouche. As a third daughter she felt "really left out, neglected, and foggy. So I developed a strong stubborn streak. I was aggressive and at the same time very dependent and weak, in a classical 'female' way."

In high school, LaRouche remembers, she had problems. "I got rebellious," she says, after being the top student in her younger years. She had no career plans: "I didn't give it any thought. Nothing. I assumed I would marry. I was always involved in romance and men. But I couldn't stay in a relationship."

After her graduation in 1943, she entered New York University. It was during this time—she pigeonholes it as a period of pseudo independence—that "I met someone, a lovely guy, who I married. Then he was sent off to the War." Upon his return from World War II, the newly wedded couple finally lived together, and had difficulties; the marriage lasted for a few months. "I ended it all," says Janice, pensively. Her ex-husband, a Salk

Institute scientist, is remarried, and LaRouche admits she still considers him "a wonderful person. It was sort of an accidental good choice except I was too dumb to know it."

After her divorce she moved to California, attended UCLA, dropped out, and lived for a time on the tuition money her parents sent her. "It was rebellion. I think it saved me. Without it I would have never emerged as a person." Eventually returning home from California, she again attended NYU, and "this time I did very well." She did not graduate, however; accepting her parents' money bothered her. It was during this time and her California experience that she held a series of "nothing jobs," as a waitress, worker in a tire-manufacturing plant, sewing-machine factory laborer, secretary, bookkeeper.

She met her second husband, a management consultant, while working in New York City. They married and lived together for eight years. A child was born two years after the marriage when Janice was thirty-two. About this spouse LaRouche says: "I wasn't really a good people-reader." But she was, she feels, a fine mother.

"I took the responsibility for an infant very well, considering where I was. I was emotionally immature, even at the time I married [for the second time]. I was really a Late Bloomer in *every* sense. Nobody grew up later than I did. I guess a lot of women don't find their own personhood until their thirties and forties. I personally had a tough time. I really did. I made so many mistakes. I *was* childish." She recalls arriving home from the hospital, after her child's birth, with a cold. She tried to get help. "And I couldn't. And I remember lying there saying to myself, 'Now here we are.
Two babies. Somebody's got to be the mother.' I said it consciously and I made the decision to be his mother. And I took to it well. I got out of bed. I got over the cold. I never got another cold. I made a decision to grow up."

She was thirty-seven when she separated from her husband and began working, supporting Daniel, and says she was never

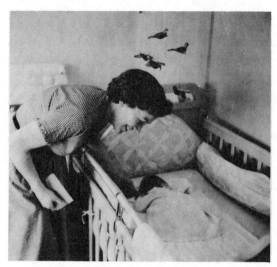

The new mother, soon to divorce.

sick. Time away from work was Danny-related: *"His* measles, *his* chicken pox. Danny was my first real project and I handled it extremely well. I had to work or die; I guess some women choose dying." She considers going on welfare analogous to death.

The depression Janice felt as her marriage deteriorated ended at the time of the separation. The child gave her a sense of self. "I became ambitious; I wanted some kind of career. I took a quick look around." She could not go to college, care for her son, and work. "You can do two of the three, not all three. Unless you don't care what happens to the child." At first, her responsibilities and lack of training boggled her. She was still somewhat immature—"intellectually, in terms of interests, emotionally, in terms of my own stability, in terms of relating, making friends." Yet she recognized her problems. Her definition of creativity is, "If it doesn't work, you try another way. That's how I started getting successful."

Looking at job opportunities, LaRouche discovered that one could become a volunteer services director—that is, in charge of the volunteers within an organization such as a hospital—without credentials, through experience. This became her goal. With investigation she learned that the president of the Association of Directors of Volunteer Services was also the director of volunteer services at the Hospital For Joint Diseases in New York. "I figured if I got to know her, I'd hear about the next opening for director of hospital volunteers. And that's exactly what happened."

So LaRouche became a volunteer; she arrived at the Hospital For Joint Diseases three mornings a week before the nine o'clock hour when she was supposed to be there. She worked for no pay for three months, "as the best volunteer that ever appeared at Joint Diseases for years, I'm sure. Because I had an ulterior motive." She explained, eventually, her ambition to the woman in charge, and when her supervisor heard of a paid opening for a clerk-typist under the director of volunteers at the Flower and Fifth Avenue Hospital, she recommended Janice. Just as Janice planned.

Her career was on its way. But personally, Janice says with a frown, she was limited: "I felt I had been dealt a very dirty deal. I was *so resentful,* and *so angry,*" and irritated at having to both carve out a career and support Danny, which still seemed, at times, impossible. "I didn't feel like a big strong person. You have to understand that. I really felt dependent and unable to do all the things I had to do. On the other hand, I was determined to do it. But I felt in a way that I couldn't. It took so much. . . . Rushing to work and rushing home, staying up late at night, and working and working and working, and running to work the next day. The funny thing is, I loved both jobs [taking care of her son and her out-of-home work]. I just had in my head the portrait of the idealized life. . . . I was supposed to have a husband, a nice house, and money for things." She laughs. "I wasn't able to play out the script. . . . It wasn't my expectation of life. The picture wasn't right. I think a lot of people have an idea how their life should unfold. It was hard for me to know that this actually *was* the good life. How was I to know? It's exciting to be busy and growing and doing things. What's good about sitting around doing nothing? I was becoming more powerful and growing and developing and learning. I know now. I teach it."

Her job was as an $80-a-week clerk-typist, although her boss, Verna Hillie, soon considered LaRouche an able administrative assistant. LaRouche worked hard, learned everything. In time, "I pushed for more money, better title," recalls LaRouche. But she could not advance within her job classification and therefore decided to take a job at another hospital.

Her boss, and now her close friend, Mrs. Hillie, helped her become director of volunteer services at the Jewish Home and Hospital for the Aged. While she held this position, during the years 1966 through 1968, New York City was shaken with racial disturbances. Rocks flew through the hospital's windows and the director of the hospital was frantic. He called a meeting but no ideas were produced, because, LaRouche remembers, the whole country was unsuccessfully struggling with the problem. During this period her personal outlook gradually developed: Be creative in your solutions, act independently, don't wait for leadership. Say to yourself, *"I* can come up with a solution even if a lot of important, sophisticated, clever people cannot." Analyzing the situation, she came to believe that the activists might have confused an expensive building with the state of the old, sick folks in it. According to Janice these individuals were in worse shape than the rioters, so "I dreamed up a program to introduce the neighborhood kids to the patients." She took a group of seventy children from the streets, aged ten to fifteen, and "I treated them like the fanciest volunteers. I toured them through the agency. I introduced them to the residents and the top brass. I had a luncheon for them. Then I showed them the conditions our patients were in." Before long she had her young volunteers sporting official caps and badges, pruning garden areas, making necessary items in the shop, producing theatrical performances and recreational events, pushing wheelchairs, concerned with safety and fire control, overseeing Bingo. LaRouche remembers they would steal the prizes and give them to the old people. She laughs. "They were funny." Of her experiences she says, "I trained myself to think creatively. And I use a lot of that stuff today."

The incidents of vandalism went from ten a week to one all summer long as LaRouche developed a public reputation for hospital improvement, allowing her to rise into a more prestigious and important job, a consulting position to directors of volunteer services for the 130 member agencies of the Federation of Jewish Philanthropies.

In 1968 she sent her son, then twelve, to a boarding school after his years of living in an apartment. She believed he needed to be out of the city and with men; he was enthusiastic about the change. At about this time the women's liberation movement

As assistant to the director of volunteers, her first job, LaRouche was gaining practical experience in a career area requiring no formal training.

emerged, and "the ideology of feminism always made sense to me. I was aware of that issue as a teenager." Her slow, easy laugh erupts. "I was a secret feminist." As soon as her son was in boarding school she started going out in the evening. "It was the first time in years, really." There hadn't been any men? "Not really. I was very busy taking care of my small kid, and I didn't have money for babysitters."

She attended a lecture on one of her nights out and challenged the speaker about his opinions of women. There was an enthusiastic ovation after she spoke, mostly from three members of the National Organization for Women, NOW. They invited her to attend a public-speaking instruction seminar sponsored by NOW.

At the instruction meeting, after it was her turn to try and give a talk, she recalls the hired speech coach commenting: " 'Now *that* was a perfect speech.' So the women threw out the speech coach and appointed me to be their teacher. Chairman of the speakers!" She laughs at the memory. And adds, "I am now very articulate. I really moved from the standard female in the worst sense—shy, inhibited, scared to talk—but I did spend many years listening. Then I forced myself to express myself."

From 1968 through 1970 she became deeply involved in NOW. She began to train leaders of consciousness-raising groups, and enrolled in a college sociology course that required involvement with a volunteer project fulfilling a community need. After having been a paid consultant to 130 directors of volunteer services, she was obviously overqualified to become a volunteer again. A psychologist friend suggested, as a way to fulfill the college requirement, that he and she form a group and co-lead it. Her reaction to his suggestion was that he was asking her essentially to be a volunteer surgeon. He was trained for such an undertaking, but who was she to do such a thing?

"I came up with a thought. More and more women were undoubtedly in the same boat I had been in, coming from standard female roles and having to carve out a career for themselves. And they often had as little preparation as I had had. I knew my situation was not unique, and I could probably give some help to women because I had done it."

She mentioned her idea to NOW acquaintances: the formation of a group that would be a substitute for the conference table, the golf club, social and business situations women are never exposed to and where men learn about the workplace. She told the NOW women that her co-group leader, the psychologist, would charge about $60 a month to each woman for the course. LaRouche would be involved on a volunteer basis: "I will co-lead it for free, but you *will* have to pay him." Their response: "What do we need *him* for?" ("Remember this is a group of feminists," explains Janice.) The eight women each decided to pay LaRouche $30 a month.

Within a year all eight participants "moved dramatically ahead in their careers," says LaRouche. One, for example, advanced from a clerk's position in the art department of a magazine to the director of two art departments at two separate publications. Another was torn between her radical friends' rhetoric and her own need to make a living. Through LaRouche's careful han-

A group including Betty Friedan and a bespectacled LaRouche, desegregating a New York City bar; this photo appeared in the New York Post.

dling, her niche was found; she now teaches radical anthropology at a university.

In the spring of 1970, LaRouche's counseling work was written up in a *New York Times* article, "A Women's Liberation Approach to Solving Career Problems." According to her it was the first time feminist activities were reported in a positive manner. Since then pieces with titles such as "First Aid for the Working Woman," "Are You Stuck?: How to Take Charge of Your Future," "From Housewife to Wage Earner," "A Workshop for the Career Woman," "Assertiveness Training for Women: Stand Up, Speak Out, Talk Back," written by or about her, have appeared in *McCalls's, Glamour, New York, Forbes.*

LaRouche's counseling-for-business career planning, goal setting, and job finding is done through the offering of courses, usually ten weeks of sessions for thirty women, but also private sessions, and a six-hour, $35 marathon for 250 women. Generating more than $225,000 a year, she trains 1,500 women each year, usually in her own living room with its graying white walls, soiled shades, nondescript sofa, and little overhead. She has also done workshops for corporations such as New York Telephone; her more specialized seminars are sponsored by businesses for their female employees.

Janice LaRouche's lectures cover business-related problems; during one such meeting, she sat with her women and practiced what she calls "strategizing: How not to be had. How to be assertive from day one." But she also on occasion covers such subjects as "Male/Female Relationships in Dating" or "Marriage and Sex." Recently asked, after she gave her prepared talk, "What do you do when he doesn't call after you've slept with him?" LaRouche discussed the feeling of having been victimized. Then she looked at the group staring up at her with anticipation all over their faces and added, "I'd call him up and I'd say, 'I'm disappointed that fucking fucked up our relationship.'" The roomful of women burst out laughing. LaRouche smiled, and said she would also tell the man, "I'm curious about it. I had hoped that sex would be the cement that would strengthen. . . ."

Where does Ms. LaRouche gather the information and expertise for her lectures and courses? "Don't ask me. I haven't got the background. I make it up!" Cackling laughter. "It's really funny. You know, you do this so much, you sort of get a sense of what's going to work. Even if you don't know anything."

This assertive, self-assured woman, so sensitive to others' problems, again says she was timid, babyish, and afraid when she went out into the world on her own. And then she adds with a grin, "Now I'm used to tackling the impossible."

Janice rose to her own personal challenge and is sympathetic to those who find it difficult. She speaks of women in the workplace who "can't take it. Can't tolerate it. They can't stand up to it. They dissolve." And she helps them.

A man once told her that in the world of business, men try to defeat women rather than compete with other men. LaRouche believes it. She gives males, en masse, credit for a variety of strengths, self-assurance, self-esteem. And she has trouble accepting—or maybe never considered—that males share many insecure feelings with women. She ponders and makes an astonishing admission: "Well, I really don't know men. I only know women."

She certainly does. LaRouche believes any female can do what she has done. "I was not creative. You *learn* to be creative." Each individual has it within her, but she must pull it out into the open, develop it.

LaRouche has experienced success with her Workshops for Women due, she believes, to her outlook after her divorce: "I did not devote myself to looking for a man," although she has been close to a particular "friend," a physician, for years. Her goal was a career. Of her business, she says, "This was a political activity that became a business. I really did develop a new idea. I did revolutionize career counseling, which previously was based on helping women to juggle their primary roles of mother and wife. Women were always trying to work things out within the workplace so that they could serve another need." She suggests that this is wrong, yet, when pushed, admits a difficult problem exists for women as they seesaw between a career and motherhood:

> **LaRouche:** Mothering is only a part-time temporary job.
>
> *Interviewer:* Part-time?!
>
> **LaRouche:** Well, full-time maybe for a few years. A lot of kids go to school at three.
>
> *Interviewer:* But nursery schools are only for a few hours a day. Unless you're talking about day care. . . .
>
> **LaRouche:** All right, all right. You can say it's a job for five years; if you have two kids, that's seven years; if you have three kids, that's about ten years. So it's a full-time job for ten years. But then it converts into a part-time job. For a few years. So let's say you're at it for fifteen years. You've spent the first twenty years of your life preparing for this fifteen-year job. At age thirty-five, you've got the next forty-five years to think about! I would advise a young woman just starting out to get her toehold *firmly* established in the workplace *before* she has a child, and to keep a foot in it while she has a child. Somehow. Because otherwise it can be an extraordinary high price to pay for the fun.

Janice and her son, now grown, live together in their Manhattan apartment and weekend retreat in Connecticut: "I love the time I spent with my child and I learned a lot from it. *I* grew and developed. It was the most challenging thing I've ever done. I don't think I've ever done anything more interesting. But I think women pay much too high a price. I think I would have continued with it—I would have become a professional child rearer!—if someone paid me a lot of money to do it. But it's not well paid and it's very hard to transfer those skills. And the credentials are not acknowledged, no matter how good you are at it."

Janice sees motherhood as a dead end, leaving a woman with a diminished earning capacity. "And without credentials. You've missed out on the critical years of gathering skills to bring you

Janice, in her apartment, examining her nails in a familiar gesture as she talks. Photo by Daniel LaRouche.

into your late mid-years and older age." Women start at forty, whereas men begin at the age of twenty. "It's very hard."

But Janice LaRouche did it. How? "I think a lot of women, in the position I was in, will after a few years . . . leap forward. I went in as a typist, and I studied and I studied and I studied the behavior of my boss, the conventions of the workplace [her lackadaisical voice gets louder, gaining momentum], the strategies, the politics—the *everything*. I accepted every challenge and then I suddenly leaped forward. A Late Bloomer can move faster in a way." The LaRouche leapfrog theory. And she's about to hop right into another field, as her strategy book is soon to be published, by Random House.

She muses, "I don't think it's *ever* too late to live."

How Janice LaRouche Did It

1. LaRouche's developing ambition paralleled her coming to terms with her responsibility as a mother; she chose to recognize her assets rather than bemoan her shortcomings.

2. She decided she did not require a man to be complete; she needed a career.

3. She had no credentials and could not, in her mind, concurrently attend college, work, and care for her child. So she searched for positions available to the uneducated and inexperienced, yet with growth possibilities.

4. To become acquainted with a powerful person—the president of the Association of Directors of Volunteer Services—Janice worked without pay for three months.

5. The excellent volunteer explained her ambition to become a paid volunteer services director to her boss, who ultimately recommended Janice for a position leading to her goal.

6. In her paid job, "I pushed for more money, better title," and when they were not forthcoming, she found a new position, as a director of volunteer services.

7. LaRouche's developing personal philosophy (Be creative in your solutions. Act independently. Don't wait for leadership.) led her to a solution for a riot situation—and elevated her to an important position.

8. She consistently concentrated on each boss's needs, then helped them to attain their goals.

9. "I forced myself to express myself." Not a natural speaker, she developed this necessary skill, made valuable by her years of information gathering—that is, listening.

10. LaRouche invented an innovative business and, by this time, had developed the self-esteem to implement it.

11. Creativity is something one learns, believes Janice. She made a conscious decision to recognize, then develop, her own particular talents.

2

Kinetic Kentuckians

Mary Jane Jesse was in the midst of a successful advertising career when, at the age of thirty-seven, and single, she decided to become a doctor. Today as a pediatric cardiologist she directs the division of the National Institutes of Health concerned with heart and vascular disease.

Her younger sister, Martha Jesse Radike, brought up her six children and, as a result of Girl Scout nature activities, chose, at middle age, to be a biologist-researcher. Dr. Martha Radike, grandmother and scientist, is a faculty member at the University of Cincinnati.

The Jesse sisters—independent, scintillating, extraverted—grew up in Kentucky.

Mary Jane was born in 1918; Martha followed two years later. Although there was enough to eat in their home, they were poor, "but everyone had a bad time in the thirties," recalls Martha. In spite of their modest circumstances, when the sisters were toddlers their mother purchased an expensive set of literature books for children, including *The Odyssey, The Iliad, Gulliver's Travels, Confessions of an Opium Eater,* rewritten for kids. This mother, "indeed a remarkable one," according to Mary Jane, "was turned on by all this stuff." Unworldly Mrs. Jesse, who never went past the sixth grade, read to her daughters, filling their minds. "Her curiosity, her interest in literature, about which she knew nothing! But she learned . . . and she had an *incredible* sense of humor." Mary Jane remembers the five-foot three-inch, slight, "very pretty woman" as "a fragile kind of elegant lady," and cites an example: In 1937 the family had to be rescued from their house in a boat as the Ohio River rose. Climbing into the life raft, the girls could not find their mother. "The water was by now lapping on the front steps." Finally Mrs. Jesse appeared, with her hat on "as if she were going to the theater." Mary Jane smiles as she recalls: "The man—a volunteer—stopped, looked at my mother, and swept the water off the porch steps." Ethel May then gradually proceeded into the vessel.

The elegant Mrs. Jesse and her husband were easygoing. "As a child, I don't ever remember pressure," says younger sister Martha Radike. "Mom did too much for us; she wanted us to have everything she didn't have. When I married, I had a bachelor's degree but I had never washed my own hair." And Mary Jane says, "Martha and I have congratulated each other on having been born to those two people. Somehow or another they got us set along some way of looking at things. . . . They had a tremendous impact on the way we saw the world. They were both basically optimists."

Both sisters say their parents loved each other. "I don't think there's any question about it," states Mary Jane, who recalls that although her mother was the stronger, her father was the boss in the house, a great mediator. Joseph Preston Jesse was a railroad clerk in the early 1900s who became involved in the beginnings of the unions. In 1929 the girls were nine and eleven as the Jesses moved from their small Kentucky town of Owensboro to Louisville, where Joseph, who "loved what he was doing," according to Martha, eventually became chairman of the local Louisville and Nashville Railroad employees, then vice president of the Brotherhood of Railway Clerks. If he lived now, the gregarious, practical joker "would have gone to college and done much more," says Mary Jane.

Martha and Mary Jane had their parents' well-developed

senses of humor since their teen years. They attended a Catholic girls' school on scholarships, where Mary Jane was a high school newspaper reporter and played the viola while Martha played bass fiddle. "We both wanted to major in music. We were hung up on drama and music." Mary Jane was interested in directing and had aspirations to the legitimate theater.

Although the parents could not afford to send their daughters to college, "they supported whatever we wanted to do," remembers Martha. She calls it luck that both she and her sister, as they graduated from secondary school, were recipients of the one scholarship offered yearly by the local all-woman Nazareth College.

Mary Jane Jesse wanted to go to New York City; it was her dream, says Martha. And after college, she did just that. Arranging to write a "local girl in New York" column for the Louisville *Courier Journal,* she would stay at a Manhattan boardinghouse for hopeful actresses until she ran out of money, go back home, earn more—once by hosting a Louisville radio program—then return to New York City to interview such luminaries as Victor Mature and Helen Hayes. "She never did make it, but the theater *was* her aspiration," says Martha.

It was in New York during the war years that Mary Jane got a job drawing nuts and bolts for the Curtis-Wright Corporation. Then in 1947 she began working for the advertising firm of Young & Rubicam. Excited about the position with the agency, she was soon writing informational blurbs, then sending them to radio stations, where broadcasters would interject the spots into their programs, essentially a method of free advertising for Young & Rubicam clients. Jesse developed a weekly packaged program, such as a segment of mending tips involving a sewing-machine company the advertising firm represented, without necessarily mentioning the corporation by name. "This was in the early days of acquiring free editorial time to promote products or ideas," she explains. With Mary Jane structuring and directing the project, it ultimately grew into a TV vehicle utilized mainly

Jesse, as a New York-based reporter for the Louisville Courier-Journal *in 1940, wrote: "Before going to bed Mary Jane writes a column describing the day's doings. . . . The column fairly bristles with the names of celebrities she's met. But Mary Jane sadly admits she hasn't made any progress toward becoming one herself. But hope springs eternal, tomorrow's a new day, etc."*

by women commentators. "We would also ship people around to be interviewed, that sort of thing."

By 1954 Jesse headed a division of ten Young & Rubicam people. "It was really very successful. We had a good time. As far as I know, it is still going on. I was happy as a clam. I didn't have any complaints. I had a *picnic.*" Jesse often speaks of the picnics of her life.

"I was thirty-six, living in single blessedness." And Martha remarks, "The number of times my sister almost got married . . ." Prior to World War II, Mary Jane was engaged to a man named Joseph Fontana. "We had gone together about a year. . . . It was a real bummer as far as I was concerned." The relationship ended when she received a "reverse 'Dear John' letter." Subsequently she dated "a whole lot of people."

She fell deeply in love with one, an Orthodox Jew, but the couple split when they recognized that her Catholicism and his Judaism would never mesh. He married twice after his relationship with Mary Jane ended. "Just got a divorce," muses Jesse, and he still calls her every six months or so. Recently his son said to him, "Why do you keep on moping around? Why don't you call up that lady you've been in love with all along and ask her to marry you?" He is a California urologist; she is established in Maryland. Mary Jane on the possibility of marrying in her sixties: "I think it's unlikely now."

Mary Jane Jesse never lived with a man. "Single virginity blessedness, if you can believe that!" Martha explains that Jesse's comment must be viewed in terms of their upbringing, and the times: "We did not look upon sex as being like breakfast, lunch, and supper. It was more set apart. Not another appetite. Something that belonged to the state of marriage. To live with ourselves, we had to remain strong morally. It has to do with your own self-image."

At thirty-six, Mary Jane had a positive self-image. She was financially secure—"I had saved a fair amount of money"—was comfortable in a New York City apartment, and was enjoying life.

Years before, when she had first come to New York, during the war, people were volunteering for various activities, and Mary Jane had taken a Red Cross Nurse's Aide course, partly to socialize. "Absolutely had zero interest in science. *Never* had any desire to get mixed up in it. But there it was—an organization to which you could go." And she did.

And this training had a hand in her ultimate career change. Jesse was seeing a Dr. Cushman Haagensen for a checkup on a day when the physician and his wife, Alice, were working on the logistics of a volunteer group for Haagensen's newly opened

Delafield Hospital. Statuesque, white-haired Alice Haagensen reminisces: "Mary Jane said she would help as a nurse's aide."

Mary Jane, in her deep southern drawl, remembers: "We [she, Mrs. Haagensen, and other doctors' wives] started the first volunteer group at Delafield Hospital." And it was there, in 1951, that "I got sort of titillated" by what the doctors and researchers, with whom she was becoming friendly, were doing. "I didn't know anything about any of this and as time went along, I got to thinking that it might be fun to do something different."

Mary Jane was at a point where she could think seriously about "doing something crazy. But in the fifties, women did not go traveling off to wild places alone, although I *did* entertain the thought." Instead she began to consider entering the medical field: "I ended up thinking to myself, 'Well, maybe, this would be fun.' "

Cushman Haagensen, Emeritus Professor of Surgery, author of perhaps the definitive text on breast disease, worldwide lecturer and breast cancer authority, responds dogmatically to Jesse's explanation of her professional start: "No no no no! She got into medicine because she wanted to help sick people. Her interest . . . in the beginning was not necessarily because of a scientific interest a'tall, but because she's a humanitarian first. *That's* what led her to work at Delafield Hospital [as a volunteer], where we took care of underprivileged people with cancer." Jesse was familiar with the disease; her mother had had breast cancer.

Jesse spoke with nursing school admittance people, who told her she was too old to enter their programs. Instead of feeling discouraged, Jesse decided to aim higher. If she could not enter the nursing profession, perhaps she should consider becoming a doctor. "I talked to Cushman and he thought it was absolutely elegant."

Cushman Haagensen: "In those days [the pursuit of a medical career] was much more difficult for a woman, particularly for an older woman; you would say it would be absolutely impossible. You must understand it was a hard row for her to hoe."

Jesse had no information on the difficulties of gaining admission to a medical school and speaks of being fortunate that she was naïve. "I guess I always sort of assumed that if you went after it, *whatever it was,* that you would end up getting it. And that's correct. Everyone else that I know who does that finds it works also."

This woman, who moved from Kentucky to the glamorous world of Manhattan and then took a totally new direction, talks of people who "curse the darkness; they never really believe that there could be some measure of betterment. . . . Successful people have a tendency to look back and eliminate the things that were really awful and talk about the things that were fun," as she does. "Well, if you're basically an optimist, you do disregard those things. You just go waving through the muck thinking a daffodil will spring up in front of your nose. It's crazy but there is *some* sense in that. I think the people who look upon problems as bad don't really understand that the only things that are *really* fun are solutions. That's an optimistic outlook. But that's kind of the way I feel about it. The other thing that I think probably plays a major role in all of this is luck. It doesn't hurt."

Once her decision was made to enter medical school, she concentrated on prerequisite courses. Mary Jane had taken only one science course in college, biology, and would have to go back to school for a year "at least, and to do it in that short a time would be kind of miraculous. And the first thing I really had to do was see if I could pass any of the damn stuff. I took the first term of inorganic chemistry. It was really weird. I couldn't remember how to get the x from one side of the equal sign to the other. So I hired a tutor who got me off the flight deck a little bit."

She was enthralled with the subject matter. In chemistry, "the experiments were absolutely *remarkable,* I thought." While she took the first term of inorganic chemistry at NYU night school, Jesse continued working at the advertising agency during the daytime. This went on five nights a week for a summer. As she began to get more involved with science, her enthusiasm grew.

She decided to try to gain admittance to Cornell, Harvard, and Yale schools of medicine immediately. "I applied right away. It was clear I wasn't going to spend three or four years just knocking off the requirements" by attending night and summer school. "I didn't have time to just fuss around with that." Recognizing that she had to discontinue working at the advertising agency, she did some serious thinking. "But once having decided that, everything was fine."

"I left it all to go to medical school. At age thirty-seven." Young & Rubicam's personnel records for 1955 note Jesse "Left to begin medical career."

But not quite yet. Attending school full time to fulfill more quickly the prerequisite courses necessary for medical school entrance, she was not allowed to take organic chemistry until completing the prerequisite inorganic chemistry, and she had taken only the first half of that course. But she didn't feel she had the time to take her course work in order. So Jesse undertook the second half of inorganic chemistry, comparative anatomy, and physics, all in her first semester. Then she went to another school, told them she had completed inorganic, and took organic chemistry there, on Saturday. The following term, having completed the prerequisites, she could then take quantitative analysis.

"As it turns out it really wasn't that hard. I had come to it having worked very hard." Mary Jane believes maturity makes going back to school easier. "Oh yeah. There isn't any *question* about it. I was thirty-seven and the kids were all eighteen, nineteen, and I had a *picnic!* It was just marvelous. I was a little bit of an anomaly. At that point no one at my advanced age was going to school."

She refers to herself as the world's greatest tourist, a person who relishes new experiences. Enthusiastic about, and fascinated with, all her courses, she particularly remembers how delighted she was to learn in physics that if a rock is dropped by someone ascending in a balloon, it does not fall immediately. "It goes up first and then down. Well, I thought that was absolutely extra-

ordinary." She adds, "You can see the level of my sophistication."

Jesse planned to work with patients. But through Cushman
Haagensen she glimpsed the field of medical research, and was
considering that as well when an offer was made by Western
Reserve University in Ohio. She could enter their medical school
if she would agree to specialize in medical communications after
she received her medical degree. Western Reserve wanted her in
particular because of her media background, but Mary Jane
refused the offer; she did not have enough knowledge at this
point to decide her specialty.

While Jesse was turning down the Western Reserve offer, her
NYU undergraduate adviser was saying: "I think you are barking
up the wrong tree. You'll never be able to pull this off. You're too
old." He was wrong.

She impressed a Columbia University admissions officer who
had personal discretion over the admittance of one individual,
without that choice being discussed by a committee, which surely
would have rejected Jesse. In 1955 Mary Jane was accepted to the
Columbia College of Physicians and Surgeons.

"That first year,"—Jesse uses a favorite descriptive phrase—
"was a three-ring circus." When she had gone to Nazareth College in Kentucky, Jesse had lived at home. Now, at thirty-eight,
she was to live with a totally different age group in a dormitory.
Her fellow students were mostly men, for at that time there was
indeed a quota for women. "Ten percent. And there weren't any
bones made about it." Was she the oldest woman in the class? "I
was the oldest *human being* in the class." But fellow medical
trainee, Sven Kister, recalls that the tall, slim woman "didn't look
out of place." And Kenneth Forde, a Columbia Presbyterian
Medical Center proctologist and classmate of Jesse's, remembers
that they used to give her Mother's Day cards. "She was mother
hen to all of us."

Her classmates and her professors enjoyed her easygoing personality.

Haagensen on medical student Jesse: Very outgoing. Quick. Bright.

Alice Haagensen: Thoughtful.

C.H.: A kind humanist.

A.H.: I can remember when Cushman—it must have been ten, fifteen years ago—started having fibrillation. At the hospital, I sat there, waiting, scared to death, you know. And Mary Jane came and sat with me. She just thought it'd be nice to do that. I'm sure she was very busy.

Mary Jane, who, in her sixties, intersperses her conversation with "cripes" and "out of sight," remembers those years with fondness. The first year she was ninety-sixth in a class of 120. And she was first in her class by her fourth year. "It didn't have anything to do with being smart. It had to do with one being more mature. For now [in the latter years of medical training] you were working with patients, and you were utilizing what you had learned. It was much easier for me than it was for people who came to this after a solid career of having been in school. I had already seen people die, for example. I had already had friends who were ill; I had seen sick people who were in a hospital and I didn't have the trauma the younger students experienced."

When Haagensen comments that Mary Jane breezed through her medical training, his wife counters, "Breezed through? I remember seeing her then. She had her hair cut very short and was thin and pale, *so* exhausted-looking." With good reason.

She was to graduate from medical school in June. On May first her mother became seriously ill. Then on May ninth her father had a massive stroke. She brought them both to her apartment. "That summer was a three-ring circus," followed by her internship at the Bronx Municipal Albert Einstein Medical College Hospital, and her father's death.

She began interning that fall, in 1959. And she discovered a lump in her breast. A radical mastectomy followed, and after the operation, Mary Jane went back to her internship, a tiring, grueling experience. It never entered her mind not to. Her doctor, Haagensen, says the surgery "would have frightened an ordinary person. Not Mary Jane." Then, shortly after her father's death, with her mother still ill, Mary Jane was driving to work on New York's Henry Hudson Parkway when "something was terribly wrong with my vision." Soon she was dizzy, vomiting. Mary Jane was forty-one years old when the doctors decided on an emergency hysterectomy. Today she talks lightly of this operation, in terms of the physicians "prodding around" and "jacking out the uterus," saying it was probably sensible to "take the thing out," because of her problems and her cancer history. Martha on her sister's adjustment to her operations: "Those things are not as important when you're totally involved."

Unable to bear children herself, Jesse continued to lean toward caring for infants. Her sister says that until then, Mary Jane "didn't ever have anything to do with kids." Dr. Mary Jane Jesse's internship at the Bronx Municipal Albert Einstein Medical College Hospital had been in the specialty of medicine. And after, when she went back to Babies Hospital at Columbia University Medical Center, "I knew I was going to do pediatrics."

Starting her two-year pediatrics residency in 1960, when open-heart surgery was becoming consistently successful, she became intrigued with cardiology as well, "an exciting, burgeoning time of being able to rescue really an awful lot of youngsters. Added to which, the physiology of heart disease had fascinated me all along." Dr. Haagensen: "She decided on one of the most attractive challenges, at that time particularly. This was when congenital anomalies in children were beginning to be operated on."

Dr. Jesse completed four years of medical school, one year of internship, and two years as a resident, and ended up with $9 in cash and one month's rent paid in advance. She was forty-four, and could have then set up a lucrative practice as a pediatric cardiologist. Jesse opted for further training.

To become board-certified, she had to possess the credentials that the pediatric cardiologists' organization required, including a two-year stint as a postdoctoral fellow. She could then be a board-certified specialist. "Specialists" who are not board-certified often have no specialized training other than that taught in medical school and internship. She joined a group of cardiologists at Babies Hospital as a fellow, and then put in two more postdoctoral years at Columbia with Dr. Al Fishman, who was in the Cardiopulmonary Laboratory at Columbia. She then became a faculty member at Babies Hospital and practiced with Sidney Blumenthal, Professor of Pediatric Cardiology.

In 1971 Jesse moved to Florida, following a colleague, Manny Papper, who became Dean of the University of Miami's medical school. Sidney Blumenthal was appointed Associate Dean, "and I became Director of Pediatric Cardiology down there, developed a group of which I am very proud."

Fully into her medical career, did she ever think back longingly for her advertising days? "Never. Yesterday is gone; tomorrow is much better." She adds quickly: "Yesterday is *valuable*. But I've never wanted to go back to anything."

Within her practice she was totally enjoying herself. She loved taking care of kids, who are "straight arrows. Existentialists. You're gone, you are *ruined* after you're two. At two you tell the truth. By three you learn to say 'thank you' for something you didn't want."

Jesse was satisfied with her life; she totally threw herself into her work and built a reputation. "Certain children [with congenital heart conditions] can be operated on and some can't, so you must *know* what you're dealing with," states Haagensen. "This [the knowing] became a specialty all in itself, which Mary Jane is now preeminent in. . . . Oh yes, she's well known to everybody."

After a career in pediatric cardiology dealing with patients and conducting research, Jesse now heads a National Institutes of Health section—Division of Heart and Vascular Diseases—where she oversees a $255 million budget and about 150 employees.

"I've got my problems with the bureaucracy, but there isn't any question that this is an *extraordinary* experience in terms of understanding how the government works." She savors being in a position to financially support medical questions "that people maybe haven't thought very much about, that we might be in a position to do something about. That's probably the most fun about the whole thing." As Director of the Division of Heart and Vascular Diseases, she oversees projects the old National Heart Institute controlled—and more, for Jesse is responsible for all the cardiovascular research the National Institutes of Health supports.

Dr. Jesse, ex-advertising woman, now physician, researcher, administrator, has risen to the top of her field. What about Mary Jane, human being?

"Blissfully single." (Martha says Jesse's hysterectomy and mastectomy "had no effect on her ever marrying. No. None.") Mary Jane created a pattern for herself early in her career, recognizing that an individual living alone can easily succumb to a dreary routine. For example, she lights candles at dinner and cooks a good meal for herself. And lives in pleasant, comfortable surroundings.

"I'm a blue and green person. My house is all white and orange." (Years ago Martha admonished her sister: " 'You don't have to think about sending kids to school, or worry about them getting squashed up in some accident. You only have to worry about you. Why don't you go ahead and buy yourself some furniture?' Of course, I didn't expect her to go *bananas!'*")

Today, at the age of sixty-one, Mary Jane has been living alone for over thirty years and says she likes it. She frequently goes to bed early now, and gets up at 7:30 A.M.; Dr. Jesse does not have the problems that many people do as they get older. "I can go to sleep if the world is crashing."

And Jesse knows how to relax. Because she's responsible only to herself, she can spend an entire weekend curled up, reading the complete works of Edna St. Vincent Millay, as she did re-

cently. Or Virginia Woolf. "The way they used words. *Incredible!*"
Mary Jane accentuates one word in almost every sentence and
draws it out. *"In-credible!"*

Alone, and generally pleased with her life. Is she sorry that she
did not marry, does not have children? She responds, "That
horse is out of the barn in more ways than one, my dear." Laughter, then seriousness. "Sure. Good grief, anybody'd be out of
their *tree* that really didn't want kids. But it didn't work out, so
there you are. And besides, I've got all the gratifications of being
a pediatric cardiologist late in the game." And marriage? She
repeats, "I think it's unlikely now." But then she adds with a sly
grin, "But who knows?"

Jesse's sister, Martha Radike—Mary Jane says Martha is her
closest friend—feels that Mary Jane's present administrative position lacks the warm relationships Mary Jane enjoyed with her
patients. And Haagensen "can't imagine Mary Jane not doing
medical work. I can't imagine her staying with this very long.
There are still many great challenges." He believes Jesse, who is
"at the top, professionally," is the physician to undertake them.
Yet when Martha is asked if her older sister is happy, fulfilled, she
answers enthusiastically, "Oh *yeah.*"

                            *   *   *

Mary Jane Jesse has firm and deep ties with the Radikes, her
only close relatives. For years, she has traveled to Martha's frantic, busy, alive home for the Christmas holidays, and at other
times throughout the year.

If there ever was a contrast to Jesse's quiet, smooth, orderly
existence, it is her sister's home and life style. The Radike family
lives in an older, somewhat dilapidated neighborhood of Cincinnati. Although Arthur Radike, a research dentist, was financially
successful in his career, he and his wife considered it important
for their children to grow up in an integrated (80 percent black)
neighborhood, with little emphasis on material possessions.

The grass is long and filled with dandelions around the Radike's

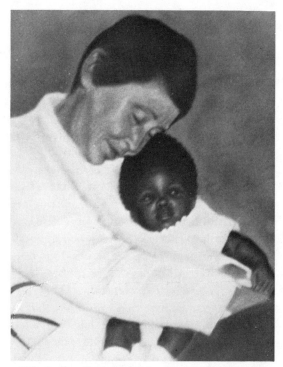

"Physically affectionate? Mary Jane?" comments her nephew rhetorically. "She can be, let me tell you. But she's not a sloppy-lipped aunt." This oil painting of Dr. Jesse hangs in the University of Miami's Jackson Memorial Hospital.

comfortable-looking, ramshackle house, which needs paint. Dogs and cats run on the four acres surrounding the house, and there is a garage-barn, which looks as if it's about to collapse, behind the house. Their old car, a disaster, sits before it.

Inside, the general shabbiness continues. The large, comfortable kitchen—one of the Radike sons proudly states he and his father redid it—has absolutely nothing that matches anything else, in style or color. Strange-looking mobiles hang here and there from the ceiling, and in one corner of the room numerous cardboard boxes, filled with papers, pamphlets, and booklets, sit on the worn floor.

"This room flooded over a year ago. I haven't done anything about it," says Arthur Radike as he enters the dining room. Throughout the house there is evidence of this benign neglect, a lack of importance attached to decorating, and a feeling of hominess and comfortable living. The Radike homestead is a contrast with Dr. Martha Radike's neat, orderly biology laboratory at the University of Cincinnati.

Martha considers herself a fortunate individual. "I've had one whole life, raising a family. And I had a pretty good slice of life even before then. And here I am starting on another one." Husband Arthur listens carefully to his wife's low voice, with its touch of the South. When asked what encouraged his wife to start anew, while the woman down the street does not, he looks surprised: "Well, you've got me! You got me! Maybe it's partly a touch of heredity, a touch of circumstance."

It was circumstance that found Martha, after graduating from college two years behind her sister Mary Jane, working at a Seagram's distillery. World War II was on, and she and a fellow employee, Arthur Radike, were involved with the manufacture of industrial alcohol for wartime purposes. "I remember the first time we were attracted to each other," he says in his soft, deliberate voice. Was she good-looking? "Well, of course, I thought so." He speaks of being overwhelmed and talks of her vivaciousness. "Martha had everything. She was full of fun, intelligent, and had a good sense of humor, a good sport—*everything.*" A delightful individual, a mature, deep thinker. "The fun, the sense of humor were just extras. She was a good person. And those things together—unbeatable." And that is how she strikes another woman: that old-fashioned phrase "of fine character."

Martha and Art are an unlikely-looking couple. She's five feet, ten inches, and he, with Mickey Rooney's stature and voice quality, seems dwarfed by her. Martha entered marriage, in 1944, having never sewn, cooked, ironed. "He must have loved me very much. It must have been terrible for him." He grins, "Naw. I was in love." He adds that now they are both lousy housekeepers. "If

you can't beat 'em, join 'em." Martha has since "learned to sew
and I've learned to can and I've learned to garden." Neither
spouse registers any complaints.

As they married, Arthur was inducted into the army and began
his first year of dental school while there. Martha quit her Seagram's job and moved with him to Columbus, Ohio, where she
worked as a lab technician until her first pregnancy.

After their daughter Jean was born, "Martha wanted to do
something," according to her husband. So when the symphony
in Columbus, previously an amateur group, went professional,
Martha, who had played bass fiddle part time in her hometown
Louisville symphony, was offered a full-time position. She loved
it, and, Art says, "The money came along as a bonus." Practicing
half of the day while her daughter was in nursery school, Martha
arrived home to care for the child in the afternoons. The concerts
themselves were in the evening, when Art could stay home with
the baby.

The family moved to Cincinnati in 1947 when Martha was
seven months pregnant with her second child. She played with a
community symphony there "for fun" and occasionally joined
Cincinnati's professional Hamilton Orchestra as a paid per-
former. "She had her hands full," recalls Arthur. "The kids were
coming pretty regularly by then."

After daughter Jean's 1945 birth, Paul was born in 1947, 1950
brought Mary Ann, Ellen in 1954, Carol in 1956, and finally, in
1957, Steven.

Martha was busy. She still occasionally played with local sym-
phonies for enjoyment. And, her husband remembers, "She was
president of the PTA, Women's Dental Auxiliary president, Girl
Scout Day Camp, Heart Association. . . . She was a Girl Scout
leader for many years and very good at it, and we all enjoyed it
a lot. She got into Girl Scouts as a lot of parents do," because
their daughter becomes involved, "but she stayed in it after the
kids were past it."

The busy mother was left alone as her husband again entered

the military, this time during the Korean War. They were then living in their present home along with cows, chickens, rabbits, geese, guinea hens, and pigs, and the "whole damn four acres were planted," remembers Art. They raised their own meat and vegetables. And the children. Martha had little free time.

Arthur was out of the service now, and his career required trips. Martha: "He traveled an awful lot." Art: "She was on her own an awful lot," as her dentist husband "set up contracts, monitored projects at universities for Procter and Gamble in my field of specialty, which is clinical research in dentistry." Arthur Radike's sister-in-law says he is the man who developed Crest toothpaste; his main responsibility was to incorporate the stannous fluoride into a dentifrice. He agrees. "I had everything to do with the development of Crest. That was my baby."

And the six babies at home were Martha's responsibility. "I had a picnic! That was fun. I enjoyed being home." She also made Christmas gifts, crocheted, tried Swedish embroidery, textile painting. "And always music."

As the six Radike children began entering school, Martha found her days were no longer totally taken up with child-related activities. (Martha remembers saying to Art: "What do I do now? I know! I'll become a good housekeeper." And his cryptic response: "Why start now?") So the house was empty, yet it became no neater or cleaner, because, Martha says, she "was soon busier than a bird dog. I was spending hours on the telephone convincing women to do things they didn't want to do, at the same time listening to the backaches, change-of-life problems, aunts, uncles, children problems. It was silly. And I wasn't happy." This is unusual for her: "I'm sort of happy-go-lucky. Things usually don't bother me. I'm not a worrier. I'm a Pollyanna. But I was unhappy. I was doing things I didn't want to do.

"I never will forget the happiest afternoon of my life. I sat down and called all these committees I was on, and I said, 'I'm going back to school.' That was fabulous. I felt a weight was lifted." It was the year her sister completed her pediatric cardiology postdoctoral studies at Columbia.

"I had talked about going back to music school," but she decided it was too late at forty-five. The time and effort involved to be a true professional was not appealing. "And, if you get arthritis in your fingers, you're sunk. But if you do something involving your *head,* if the rest of your body gives up on you, you're still all right."

Art also remembers these beginning steps of his wife's scientific career. Not a talkative man, he can't say enough about his woman's accomplishments. In his slow and understated way: "She was up to her ears in Girl Scouts, PTA, and I don't know how many other things, almost a full-time job. But her activities were so miscellaneous that it was not as fulfilling as a full-time job." Art thinks back: "It was about a week after school started [their youngest, Steven, was then in the second grade]. She called me up and said, 'Guess what? I quit all my jobs. I'm going back to school.' " Martha Radike had decided, without any conversation with her husband. She didn't mention it the night before, the week before. "That's how it was presented to *me,* " states Art, and Martha inserts, "It's hard to say it was a one-day decision. It all came about in about a week. The buildup."

"When I went through all those pregnancies, I planned, when all the kids got into school, to be a volunteer in a hospital. I was going to stay with women in labor. The period when we had our children was when they didn't allow husbands in with the wife. . . . But I didn't do it. I didn't do that."

Martha says today that she "got so much satisfaction out of twenty years of Girl Scouting, I miss it." And, in fact, scouting caused this woman to get onto the track of a late-blooming career.

The Radikes, in connection with her Girl Scouting activities, had "gotten very interested early on as a family in fossil hunting" on the hillsides around Cincinnati. "It's an unusual area" geologically. They also enjoyed identifying wildflowers, and they were bird watchers. "My idea of biology was, 'What is it?' " says the ex-nature lady at Girl Scout Day Camp, referred to there as "Flipper." "A big bird with a big bill and a big nose." Although she did not take biology in high school or in college—"I was a mushy, goopy softie for animals. I didn't want to dissect them" —she knew she loved biology after her scouting and family adventures. After bringing up a slew of kids a mother is either going to love it or hate it, believes Martha. And she loved it.

After her pronouncement to her husband—"I'm going back to school"—Martha went to the head of the University of Cincinnati's biology department. "I said, 'Is it crazy for a forty-five-year-old woman to consider going to graduate school in biology if she's never had a course in biology?' " She first had to complete an undergraduate major in biology, although she already had a bachelor's degree, and the department chairman was extremely encouraging. He suggested taking a full load rather than a few courses, totally immersing herself. "So that's what I did. I signed up for entomology, and I didn't even know what it was.

"But I didn't go back to school with a goal, to become a whatever. I went because I felt I was wasting my time, and I think that's essentially why Mary Jane got into medicine. I went back because I thought I would enjoy it. I didn't think I was doing anything that was needed, necessary, important."

Her enjoyment with her first courses affirmed the correctness of her decision. It's said that going back to school when one is older is difficult. "Baloney. I think it's easier." There is no concern about looks, falling in love, "all the things that assail a young person." She recalls, "I went back when I was forty-five and was amazed at the nervousness of the college student. . . . But if I failed, boobity-doo, so what? It would only be my pride. It wouldn't be my whole life." There was no financial pressure with her husband supporting her. "That's quite true. And also, I remembered when all those things weren't known. And so it wasn't something I had to learn; it was *fascinating.*" For example, when she took biology in 1965, a discussion on DNA came up. "The kids were grumbling that they had to memorize it. But to me, it wasn't something that had to be learned so I could crank it out onto a sheet of paper. It was *tremendously* exciting!"

Martha, like her sister, seems to find a word in every sentence worthy of emphasis.

And again like her sister, she enjoyed school, as she relishes all her life experiences. Although serious when it is appropriate, Martha is a joy to be around, as she seeks out the best moments a woman knows and capitalizes on them. It leaves her a funny, introspective person, as is Mary Jane. "I think," says Art, "the crux of the thing is that I don't ever remember Mary Jane clowning, and Martha loves to clown. She embarrasses her teenagers." Martha laughs, and suddenly says to her guest: "Did you give productions when your children were little? Did you enjoy having an audience?" She, who obviously did, recalls playing the role of Carmen, with rose in mouth. She kiddingly retorts: "I wasn't acting *silly*. I was putting on an opera for the children with the record playing!"

Art interjects, "I'm a perfect counterpart for this kind of thing. *I'm* not nutty." But he certainly is unconventional. It was his idea —and she concurred—that his first decent paycheck be spent on a pair of binoculars to bird-watch, at a time when they were, says Art, "loaded with kids, debts." Martha recalls, "And I was washing clothes in the bathtub!"

The two—a Mutt and Jeff combination—so obviously like and love each other. "If I ever get to heaven," says Art, "it'll be because I married her." He says it did not annoy him when Martha started her career. Yet one of their six offspring recalls, "She'd start to get home later and later, and Dad"—who is defined by his children as head of household—"would be pretty bothered by that. But it doesn't bother him any more." Actually it turned out, says Art, that with his wife in school, "we had more time together. Although it wasn't the same kind of time . . . because she was always studying." They were in the same house at least.

"And I plowed through," says Martha. "I'm not a brain. I'm a hard worker." She remembers the day a professor asked: "Is there anyone in this lab who has never used a microscope?" Only one. "Boy . . ."

She did well scholastically and completed the requirements for the equivalent of a BS in a couple of years. Art recalls, "By the time she had her master's, she was hooked" on studies.

"I did not start out to get a PhD." But at some point a career in research and university teaching looked great, and in 1974 the fifty-two-year-old woman became Martha Radike, PhD. "Got a lot of satisfaction out of that."

Art, mature and assured, delighted in his wife's accomplishments. But what would a woman do if wed to a less accommodating husband? Martha ponders, then says to Art: "Dr. Frazier, for one, has said he would like to meet you because he can't imagine a husband allowing his wife to do this. He said you must be a really super guy." Art: "I don't see any big thing in it, as long as you're enjoying it." But what *about* the difficult husband who absolutely refuses to "allow" his wife to do such a thing? Martha: "Well, you'd work it out. Women appear to me to complain a great deal more than men."

There was indeed a time when Arthur did not wish her to work. Arthur: "You were raising a family, and I'd rather raise my family under modest circumstances than to have my wife go out and share the earning burden. It's a decision on what kind of living standard you have to have. And it should be a joint decision." He looks around his house, turns to his guest, and chuckles. "As you can see, that's never bothered us."

Not much flusters them, on any level. It is difficult to get him to state what about Martha irritates him: "You learn to avoid those things."

This marriage works; the family is close. When asked which child takes most after his wife, Arthur, after heavy thought, says, "None of them." Their children—the older ones are in their thirties—include a dentist daughter who is a divorced mother, a college dropout, a biology major interested in crop science, a will-o'-the-wisp, a California natural-foods freak, and a car sales-man.

Their youngest son, Steve, when asked to describe his mother in one word, is cut off by her chiming in, "If you say 'fat,' I'll kill you!" Steve laughs, ponders. He can't describe her in *one* word: "Alive, vivid, vivacious. Honest, loving, fun-loving. Crazy-good, different. Different, for sure."

Martha's ties to her adult children continue to intertwine with her career. On the way to the lab, she drops off a daughter's stereo; Mother forgot it in the trunk of her car among some research papers. In the middle of cooking dinner, she'll walk over to the kitchen blackboard to chalk an organic chemical structure for her visitor, right next to the message her husband left for her, signed "Love Art," and the "Smoking can eat your lungs alive" sign (Dr. Radike's research involves toxic inhalants).

Martha no longer takes a midday rest on the floor—where she could be sure she was too uncomfortable to fall asleep—in be-tween caring for six children. But she does do housework at one

The Radike family in 1972, with Martha, standing, at center and Art, standing, at right. Once, when some extra cash suddenly became available, a family meeting was held to choose which drastically needed house repair to tackle first. The unani-mous decision—to build a swimming pool.

A.M. She loved the hectic mothering years and she is happy today, as a scientist: "I think change is good, professionally and personally. I like *doing*. I could undoubtedly be happy being many things. But I really like young people the best. I think that is one of the reasons I loved going back to school. And I enjoy teaching very much; I find it extremely satisfying." Her research-teaching position is not stressful; pressure is self-imposed only, and Martha believes that this kind of self-discipline is absolutely necessary for the scientist. In a medical program or law school, a structured program exists. Nobody wishes the student to deviate from that. But to earn a scientific PhD, "you've got to be hooked or you won't make it," for doctorate programs require individuals to think for themselves. They must become excited, enthusiastic with their own research. Like Martha.

Presently involved in the budding field of inhalation toxicology research—she studies the effects of inhaled toxic agents "on the bod"—Martha conducts experiments, often using laboratory ani-

Fun-loving Mary Jane once dressed Martha (then an at-home mother) in a lab coat and introduced her at the hospital as a dermatologist. In 1979, Radike wears her own white jacket in her University of Cincinnati laboratory.

mals, with the help of assistants. She writes her experiments up into articles for scientific journals. Often she travels to scholarly meetings, where she presents her results. She has had her professional career for some six years and says, "I'm getting better known." Her sister, Dr. Jesse, says Martha has an excellent reputation in the field.

* * *

Dr. Haagensen has just finished explaining the difficulties a 1950s woman—such as Mary Jane Jesse—encountered when attempting to enter medical training, and, following that, the strenuous work involved, night after night. His wife has asked Haagensen why, then, he encouraged Mary Jane if it was all so hard? He shoots back: "We *need* people like that, my dear. She was such an intelligent woman, of course, and an able woman, highly motivated, of complete integrity and with character. They don't grow on trees."

Alice turns to their visitor, and interprets her seventy-nine-year-old spouse's remarks: "Cushman's general feeling is that women are better off in the home and having children. Yet, he admires and likes all the woman doctors he knows very much."

Cushman: "No, that's not fair. My dear, somebody's got to bring up the children in life. And men aren't generally able to do it, or do it as well. But if you have someone who is as highly motivated to get into medicine as Mary Jane, that's where she *ought* to be." He pauses, then adds, "Women are more enduring and more able than men, quite often."

Alice: "Yes, Mary Jane was a person who knew what she wanted, and did it."

College student Steven Radike: "My mom did so much. And at her age!"

And Art, who sometimes calls Martha "Mama," "softened up," according to their youngest child. "It used to be that Mom'd try to put everything around Dad." It has changed. Now it is Art who writes the checks, putters in the garden, does the shopping. He now stays home, retired, as his wife goes to work.

Martha's youngest says his mother and her sister can both be very businesslike, "but they can be loose, too. Flexible. . . . They're so much the same; they both wanted to do something where they could use their minds." Dr. Jesse, Administrator, pictured at the National Institutes of Health.

Life has entered a new passage for Art and Martha. "I'm getting the wrinkles, the saggy-baggies, and other things," she says. A question for Martha: Do you think you'll ever retire? "Unh-unh!"

All is well in the Radike household.

How Mary Jane Jesse Did It

1. She made a conscious decision to enter the medical field. And when told she was too old for nurses' training, she aimed higher and decided to become a doctor.

2. Jesse needed a mentor, someone in the medical field who believed she could change careers. She found one, in Cushman Haagensen.

3. She conquered her first chemistry course by hiring a tutor, "who got me off the flight deck a little bit."

4. Jesse says it wasn't hard to take double the amount of prerequisite courses: "I had come to it having worked very hard."

5. Instead of complaints, excuses, and depression, Mary Jane was fascinated, enthusiastic, and optimistic, expecting a daffodil to spring up in front of her nose.

6. Two serious illnesses did not deter her; she had a goal.

7. After seven years of medical training, the forty-four-year-old Dr. Jesse, ignoring her age, opted for even more advanced training.

8. The physician-administrator, who continues to rise to challenges, says some "curse the darkness; they never really believe that there could be some measure of betterment." Not Mary Jane Jesse.

How Martha Radike Did It

1. Martha Radike raised six children, often with husband Art absent, and totally enjoyed it.

2. Her love of scouting led to the realization that she was fascinated with biology.

3. Considering her options, she decided against a late-blooming musical career and chose science.

4. Radike resigned from her volunteer activities, realizing that the hours involved were the equivalent of a full-time career.

5. At forty-five, with her youngest child in second grade, she took the biology chairman's advice and signed up for a full load of courses, immediately becoming totally involved.

6. She found college easier as a mature adult. Under no financial or personal pressure to succeed, she was becoming further educated simply because she wished to.

7. Her husband supported her ambitions.

8. Martha has had the best of two worlds, in her opinion. The wrinkles and saggy-baggies don't bother this investigator/teacher; she sees her life as beginning again.

3

Galloping Gloves

At the end of the hallway is the gray-carpeted Department of Labor seminar room, filled with four long rectangular tables set in a square. Upon one of the upholstered chrome chairs sits Marjorie Bell Chambers, a figure with disorganized reddish hair and wearing an ultrasuede suit in a neutral color. Women—and one man, the committee's counsel—walk about, discussing an afternoon ERA conference, problems with Section 3 of a federal act, possible legislation involving Title IX. "Here's a draft of an executive order, Greta. We could adopt it 'subject to.' " The blond woman being addressed nods her head.

An abundance of southern drawls permeates the air as reporters and others sit quietly, against the walls. At the head of the table is former college president Chambers, with a gold ERA stickpin on her lapel, her wrists heavy with silver Indian bracelets and turquoise jewelry about her neck. Visually reminding one of a WASP schoolmarm, she is unexpectedly cool, relaxed. She laughs easily. As acting chairperson of the regular bimonthly meeting of the National Advisory Committee for Women, she speaks dogmatically when necessary and remains in control. Now she uses her hands for emphasis, pointing a turquoise-and-silver-ringed finger, symbolic of her New Mexico home. Now she sits listening, her rounded shoulders leaning forward, her expression and neck angle reminiscent of a cautious dromedary. She looks

45

down, takes a note. Her piercing eyes stare at the black woman
who has the floor, then shift to the Oriental woman across the
table. She blinks frequently; her contact lenses are irritating her
eyes, she says, because of the dirty Washington, D.C., air, so
different from her Los Alamos environment. Chambers nods her
head, a stern expression on her creased face. As she rubs an ear,
her hair becomes more mussed; she has been busy throughout
the day and has not recombed it.

One of the group of well-dressed articulate women sums up a
long discussion. Chambers, talking through her teeth: "It seems
your suggestion is the better one, the least time-consuming." A
moment later, practical Dr. Chambers reminds committee members to keep track of their expenses: "You can take it off your
income tax." If she's discussing something and is interrupted, Dr.
Chambers goes right back to her subject. (Her slightly pompous
explanation: "I'm a historian!")

A discussion of possible Social Security revisions reveals that
a divorced woman's Social Security benefits increase when her
ex-husband dies—in fact the amount becomes twice as much as
she received while he lived. Under her breath Chambers mutters
a cynical solution to the problem: "Poison him."

With no discernible makeup except a thin line of lipstick across
her face, she looks tough and capable in her role of advising the
President of the United States. The impression is correct.

The meeting over, she whisks off in a chauffeured limousine to
an ERA briefing, where as national president of the 190,000-
member American Association of University Women, she pins on
an "AAUW for ERA" badge, then takes her place at yet another
squared table arrangement, about a dozen seats from Betty Friedan. She leans with elbows on the white tablecloth, her back
hunched. Hard of hearing, she listens carefully.

"What we want is equal access to jobs." Her head nods, her
thin sinewy figure shifts. The young woman next to her wears
a badge, "Mormons for ERA." NOW President Eleanor Smeal
stands up and speaks: "We intend to create *such a political cli-*

mate . . ." Marge's shrewd half-smile makes her eyes form small slits. *". . .* women are not going to *crawl* into the Constitution; they're going to *march, proudly!"*

The briefing is over and the delegates walk to another area within the hotel for a press conference. Chambers' energetic wide stride is faster than any of them; her eyes appear to be set on the horizon a mile and a half away although she is only going down the hall into another conference room. Heavy eyebrows, jutting out over her sockets, add to this forward-looking impression.

As soon as the press conference is over, a woman lobbyist, representing the California System of State Colleges and Universities, meets with Chambers to discuss the AAUW's lack of male members. Chambers speaks firmly, decisively.

The University of California representative completes her comments and it is time to go onto the streets of Washington. Chambers says she has a fine sense of direction. She lopes along, now startlingly resembling a greyhound, her eyes again fixed on some invisible distant point.

Her whole being seems to be epitomized in her walk—an advance, a strong-willed force, a progression, a mobilization. This galloping attitude propelled Marjorie Bell Chambers into her present variety of positions.

From her birth in 1923, elements and pieces of her late-blooming life were set in place, at first by Marjorie Louise's father, Kenneth Bell, born to British missionaries in Angola and raised in Toronto. He later moved to New York City, where he was a banker with first the Chase National, then the Chase Manhattan Bank. Marjorie's mother, Katherine Bell, was, according to her daughter, "basically a homemaker but she was also an artist." Charcoals, pastels, a bit of oils. "And she was my father's official hostess, and a very charming woman. We had a beautiful home, which reflected her artistic taste. She was a typical kind of corporate wife who saw her function as enhancing her husband's position. And she did it very well. He was proud of her. She was a very handsome woman. She had a sparkle. . . . He had the mate that he wanted and needed. Except in an intellectual sense. They never had in-depth conversations. He was an exceptionally brilliant man.

"My parents really did have a stereotyped division of labor. Mother taught us the social graces, if you want to call them that, and Dad was the intellectual. I was the oldest [her sister is seven years younger] and he had no sons and I think I became the son he never had. From the crib he was trying to get me accustomed to foreign languages. Did he do the same with my sister? No."

Marjorie was the sickly, anemic child. She attended private school sporadically, but most of her learning came from her father's tutoring. In spite of missing a tremendous amount of school, she skipped the second grade. "Then I was out of my social group, as they say." Finally her illness was correctly diagnosed as tuberculosis and "my father was told to get me out of the city or I wouldn't survive, so we left New York and went to Scarsdale." There she became a triple letter winner—hockey, basketball, tennis. Although the young girl was involved in sports, she was still withdrawn. One teacher helped by requiring students to memorize dialogues from Shakespeare plays. "You had to give the next line in the play, and somehow I learned to talk on my feet. It was pure torture. But I don't think I've ever had trouble speaking since," she says in her hoarse voice, a touch of New Mexico in her language. "It gave me the self-confidence so many women say they don't have." Her high school interest in skating helped change her introverted tendencies also. "Being able to stand up and speak, and being able to take off and dance to music on the ice—and have people watch!—the two gave me a kind of self-confidence we now see women getting in self-assertiveness training. I had that pretty early."

One of Marjorie's skating partners was William Chambers, a year older than she. They dated each other casually until Bill left for Cornell, and it was time for Marjorie to go to college.

Although Kenneth Bell helped with his daughters' homework,

it was his uneducated wife who insisted on college for her children. "She never had her college training, and I think she missed it" and wanted the advantage for her children.

Upon Marjorie's graduation from Mount Holyoke College, her father guided her toward the Katharine Gibbs School, a one-year course for executive secretaries. "He put it in the frame of an insurance policy. He said I would always be able to eat if I was a secretary." Her father imagined his oldest daughter would marry and have children, "that was there too." But Katharine Gibbs was insurance.

Bill Chambers graduated from Cornell and entered the service as Marjorie started at Gibbs; then, upon completion of the executive secretarial course, in 1944, she started to work as Bill went overseas. Marjorie's position was as exciting as Bill's war experiences.

Working in Manhattan for the League of Nations Association (later renamed The United Nations), "I took down the Dumbarton Oaks Proposal in shorthand, on the telephone from Washington. And from then on, it was just bedlam in that place. I had been hired as the contest secretary. They would have essays on how wonderful the League of Nations was and so forth," but once the proposal was created, "I put on big conferences. . . . I dealt with radio and press, setting up interviews. I wrote publicity. Different companies would lend their experts to train the League's staff. It was a most exciting time to be there!"

She left one week after the United Nations charter was ratified, in 1945.

Bill Chambers had returned from overseas, and while the couple unsuccessfully tried to help engaged friends patch up their romance, Marjorie and Bill found "we had fallen in love," and married. He wished to become a physicist and started graduate school at Cornell in upstate New York, where Marge was hired as the sociology department stenographer at $100 per month. Her organizational ability and her quick mind were put to use. "In short order I was running the whole rural sociology depart-

ment, I was doing the farm and home radio program hours. I ran
three, four loan libraries for the countryside, plays they started
in the Home Extension Club. I wrote program pointers for everybody, 4-H, extension clubs. And finally I got mad.

"I went in to the professor—who was a woman. My two bosses
were women, which is interesting. The first one never confined
me to shorthand. She saw I could do other things. And this other
one, the same thing. She made use of me. I even corrected her
students' papers. A stenographer correcting her professor's papers! Anyway, I finally walked in and I said, 'I think there's something unfair about this system. I'm being paid to be a stenographer and I'm not so sure I'm not doing a professor's job.' She
says, 'Of course you are. Get over there to the Graduate School
and enroll. I was waiting for you to rebel.' "

She went to the History Department, which was unwilling to
give her any financial support: " 'Women aren't historians,' they
said." Through her ex-boss in the sociology department she
obtained a research fellowship, exempting her from the $2,000
tuition. This could have been awarded by the history department,
where she was enrolled, but "they said I'd just get pregnant."

And she did. But she miscarried. She became pregnant again
and "I was eight months pregnant when I took my orals." Her
two male examiners were "like mother hens. When I was
through, *they* went out into the hall to discuss it rather than ask
me to step out. So I knew I had passed. . . . I got my master's and,
a month later, I had my first child, in 1948."

Two months later she, her husband (with his master of science), and the baby moved to Columbus, Ohio, where Bill taught
at Ohio State University while earning his doctorate. A second
child was born while the Chambers lived in Ohio, as Marjorie
earned extra money preparing theses and term papers: "I just sat
there typing with two babies crawling around me."

In 1953 Bill was hired by the Atomic Energy Commission in
Los Alamos, New Mexico, a town of 18,000. The company town
is, says Marjorie, "a 'sub' without an 'urb' to be 'sub' to. But it

has all the aspects of surburbia." Marjorie was anxious to continue with her historical career but there was no graduate school for a hundred miles. "The conducive factors weren't there, and the screaming children were there. But what I did was, I read. My children knew that they did not disturb me between one and three. They took their nap and then, if they woke up, they could play in their beds and in their room. But from one until three, Mother read history. And I did. I kept up with my professional societies, I kept up with my reading." Preparation for her inevitable career.

"And right away, I became involved in Girl Scouting. I had a troup of thirty-four girls. I said I'd lead it if the mothers would babysit for my two kids. My kids spent time with a different mother every week, and I decided that it was a very good experience for them."

But, aside from this organized babysitting, "I had absolutely no relief from their care. My husband was working six days a week, or he went out into the Pacific for tests, or he went to Nevada for tests. And those kids were only eighteen, nineteen months apart. And there was no grandmother, there were no babysitters. You could give them to a friend to take care of. But then I had to turn around and take care of the friend's kids. There were times when the first two were small when I was tensed up. But every time I moaned and groaned about my two, I'd say to a friend, 'How can you manage six?' and she'd say that after the third, the first two were a lot easier."

Marjorie found that out as the babies kept coming. After the birth of daughter Lee in 1948 and son William in 1949, daughter Leslie arrived in 1953 "I think I was subtly giving the girls names that would not necessarily say they were women. I knew that women writers who wrote under female names were not generally as well accepted as males who wrote similar things under male names." Kenneth was born in 1956.

"After I had the third one, the first two *were* a lot easier. . . . I stayed home for fifteen years. Should women stay at home with children? I wouldn't recommend it beyond the time they go to public school." Earlier than that, "It depends upon the child care available. A loving parent doesn't have to do it twenty-four hours a day." She speaks of the advantages of a live-in grandmother. "So I don't want to say all women should stay home. It depends upon the arrangement. But I wanted to play a major role in those first five years of my children's lives, determining their value structures and behavior patterns."

"There really wasn't any relief unless I went to the American Association of University Women's Study Group Meetings where, again, I would be exchanging babysitting with somebody." Her deep involvement with AAUW began when she saw a notice:

> All women graduates of colleges and universities, come to a party and find out if someone from your alma mater is in this town.

"It was an AAUW organizational gimmick, and I met five Mount Holyoke people there, all of whom joined." The Los Alamos AAUW branch was new and soon became seventy-five strong. Marjorie was active in the group that stressed intellectual growth and service to the community. "I went to every single AAUW study group there was because I was thirsty for some kind of intellectual communication." Marge became Los Alamos' AAUW president and a state board member the following year.

Then, at the age of thirty-two, Chambers became AAUW state president. She also had a baby. "I nursed them all, but once they got on the bottle, Bill would take care of them as well. He babysat when I went to meetings." She also founded a Los Alamos non-profit preschool, still in existence. And had a hysterectomy; after six pregnancies, four producing children, "the doctor said, 'Marge, quit! Your innards are falling out. You've got two boys, and two girls—what more could you want! What the hell more could you want!'" This made sense to Marjorie. "I was just playing the typical roles of middle-class suburban society."

With no new babies, she accepted more important AAUW roles, beginning in 1958, as her youngest child entered public school. "My first national position was on the International Relations Committee of AAUW," where, instead of attending study groups for stimulation, she was utilizing her history training by writing and designing packets put together by experts in a variety of fields: Nuclear Power, The American Family, Our Beleaguered Earth. And at the same time, she was active in the international relations programs.

At the AAUW International Relations Committee meetings in D.C. she was thrown in with women all of whom had PhDs, and "although they accepted me, that sort of started me with the idea again: 'I'm going to get that doctorate someday.' " She traveled to take educational courses, considered becoming a history teacher, but "before I completed the courses in May of 1965 [Marge's ability to remember dates is impressive], the Atomic Energy Commission decided they wanted a historian to write a history of the community management program in Los Alamos." Marge, at forty-two, with her master's degree in history, was hired.

As she wrote the history on a part-time basis, she attended the University of New Mexico in preparation for the earning of her doctorate degree. "I drove over fifteen thousand miles during those years, from Albuquerque and back," expanding her AEC document into her PhD thesis. "And I was still home for lunch" when the children arrived.

Her children grew older, ate lunch at school; AAUW positions became a career. "It's been very exciting for me because I was able to use all the skills I had in the organization." It enabled her to keep her foot in the professional door. "Tremendous experiences! They've sent me to Japan, they've sent me to Germany, they've sent me to Switzerland. They've sent me to Russia—and to Washington, D.C., on and off for twenty years for one reason or another." So while her children were small, Marjorie Bell

Chambers had modeled her activities into a future career. Her AAUW positions created an impressive résumé, yet excepting her part-time AEC position Chambers was, at fifty, an experienced individual solely through expenses-paid-only volunteer efforts.

In 1973 she served on the National Women's Political Caucus, lobbied for the Equal Rights Amendment at the New Mexico Legislature, and was an AAUW representative to the International Federation of University Women Council. She accepted a Visiting Assistant Professorship at Oklahoma's Cameron University. "It was Kenny's last semester in high school and I'm off living in Oklahoma. He and his father had a very close relationship that spring," as Marjorie's life began to, incredibly, become even more accelerated. In the fall of 1974 the many-times-elected volunteer administrator ran for political office. "I didn't have enough to do, just teaching!" She was elected as a member of the Los Alamos County Council. In January of 1975 "they made me chairman, in effect, of the town." Townspeople remark that she is an extremely aggressive individual. But her husband says, "I think she's not overpowering in the sense of domineering. That's the wrong picture. But she does know what she wants, what her goals are."

In 1976 she became president of the Colorado Women's College, in Denver. Bill, in Los Alamos, bought a plane and flew to Denver on weekends and sometimes during the week: "I don't think the students knew he wasn't living with me in the President's mansion. . . . Did I miss him? I can't really say that I did. I had too much to do."

An understatement. In that same year, Chambers was appointed by President Ford to the Advisory Council on Women's Education Programs, was a Department of Labor Advisory Council appointee, was an evaluation consultant to a college accrediting association, and, though a Republican, served on Jimmy Carter's Task Force on Education. Plus AAUW obligations, unpaid monetarily but valuable as experience and credentials. This pattern continued as she replaced a fired Bella Abzug as National Acting Chairperson of the President's Advisory Committee for Women.

"I'm sorry to be in my fifties because I find it an exciting time to be alive, and I think I would like to be around for another hundred years. I know who I am. I know what I want to do." She commands respect and admiration, if not always friendship. "I always wanted to be somebody. I wanted to go down in the history books. There were times I really thought, What is it a woman can *do?* I had dreams of being a foreign correspondent, that I would really make a contribution to international understanding, or a diplomat. But I discovered it was a very sexist

Chambers has been a member of the Board of Associates of St. John's College, interviewer for the Seven College Conference, school representative for Mount Holyoke College, and committee member of the Japan International Christian University in Tokyo. And between Bella Abzug and Lynda Johnson Robb, she headed Jimmy Carter's Advisory Committee for Women. The volunteer for women chats with the President, who wrote: "Thanks and best wishes to my friend . . . Jimmy Carter 1–31–79."

world." She admits to using all available methods as she built her public career, "but I think to a certain extent I've outgrown manipulation. I certainly was a manipulator at one time. Men whom I know I have threatened in the past now look upon me as an interesting person. One told me the other night, 'You've got more damn self-confidence than you need.' He was right. There it is."

Bill Chambers, sitting alone in the living room of their unpretentious Los Alamos home—as Marge jets first to California, then to the East Coast—agrees. Piles of magazines are everywhere. The house appears to be middle-class, although, in this inflationary town, it is in fact expensive.

The house is empty now except for Bill; the Chamberses' four children are adults. One is a historian at the University of Colorado, another an Albuquerque chemist. Daughter Leslie is studying physiology, and their younger son is at the University of Colorado in the physics program.

When Marge speaks of her spouse, she regularly uses the phrase "Still water runs deep." This quiet easygoing man who has picked up the western conversational cadence, spoke of his wife more than she anticipated, describing her as an "outward-looking person, very active and *very much* a doer. She's always been energetic. She's interested in getting things done." Her dominant characteristic is the desire to accomplish things. She's always reaching for goals, striving for excellence. And does she take defeat easily? "Nooo. [Laughter.] She doesn't like to lose." But she bounces back for the next round. When asked what it is that drives him crazy about her, "I don't think there's anything. . . . She has an excellent ability to pick out the major points in a discussion in a logical way. She's very articulate."

But she can't cook. "That's not been one of the more important things in our lives," Bill says. Daughter Leslie says, "She burns the coffee. She puts it on the stove and goes and types four letters. She gets very immersed in her work. Preoccupied. Somebody once said, 'What mom needs is a wife.'"

Marjorie recalls constant traveling, giving talks and then going home exhausted; several times she landed in the hospital with pneumonia. "It was because I never left the house without doing every single bit of laundry, ironing, freezing all the meals. . . . And finally I said to my husband and my children, 'Would you like Mommy to stop traveling—or is Mommy a different person because she travels?' And they all said, 'Oh Mom, you come back from your trips and you're so interesting.' I told them, 'Then you're going to have to do the washing and the cooking and the house cleaning and Mother isn't going to do it any more.' And I just quit. All I did was pack my suitcase and walk out the door and I haven't been sick since." Leslie recalls that "it didn't really bother me when Mom was gone a lot. When things didn't get done it was not a big household crisis. The rest of us learned how to do these things to the point where it was livable."

Marjorie thinks about her frequent absences and believes any husband would be happier to have his wife home. When traveling, she does not speak with her husband every day. "Nope. No news is good news. I see him when I get home. We only call for a purpose. I should have phoned him last night to tell him I found the checkbook in my purse. He'll be looking all over the house for it.

"We have not been this lovey-dovey pair who can't stand to be separated from each other." He travels also. "He's in meetings behind closed doors and secret discussions." It's not always easy to call him. But "I would say we are very close companions at this time. We ski together like mad. We play tennis. Swim together. I don't know. What do you do after you've been married thirty-four years? The intensity of a honeymoon is not still there, but if you've been through a long marriage, you've raised four children successfully—I think it's 'friend,' it's 'companion,' it's part of yourself almost. We don't go through demonstratively kittenish romantic gestures, but it's because we've lived together for so long. That's not to say it's not there, that we don't enjoy each other sexually. But somehow or another, that really isn't the prime reason that you live together after that length of time. I think it's when you first start marriage that sex is far more important. That seems to be the only relationship that you have. You're sexually attracted to each other; that's why you're married. As you get into the problems of building a home and producing the children and making decisions about them, and in the case of one daughter we had the traumatic experience of her being blinded in one eye, and we doing it to her. . . ."

For once, Marjorie Bell Chambers' voice softens. It was the summer before Leslie's third birthday. "We were looking at some land where we might build a house, and I saw a yucca plant I wanted to take home. I couldn't seem to dig it up and my husband was helping me with a penknife. And Leslie squatted down behind him. And all of a sudden the plant gave and went into her face. She was in the path of the plant and it punctured her pupil. The tip of the yucca plant has a poison in it." Leslie had two operations, and she wore a patch for years. She lost the sight of that eye. "Rather traumatic to deal with," says her mother. "You go through the experience of an injured child, losing another child in pregnancy . . .

"Three times in my life I was told I wasn't going to live any longer, once when I was a child, and twice as an adult." She was admonished to slow down. "Well I'm probably doing ten times more now, but I have definitely learned how to pace myself as well as when to just quit, go to bed and say, 'The hell with you' and sleep for two days."

Marjorie Bell Chambers, now in her mid-fifties, recognizes that she retains some of the stereotyped notions of her generation and of her parents: "I know my age and I know my period of time. And I'm not twenty, thirty, or even forty any more. With my culturalization, some of the old stereotypes of my parents' generation that were forced upon me, I still retain. Like slips. Why, my father would never answer the doorbell without buttoning his vest and putting on his suitcoat." And gloves. "Oh, I seldom wear them. They're a pain in the neck. But I still carry them." She pulls a white pair from her purse. Gloves go with her to an ERA meeting.

"With the whole women's movement, I have become more demonstrative. I frequently throw my arms around a woman whom I've been through a tense situation with. . . . Although there are times when Bill and I go dancing or we hold hands, I wouldn't say we are outwardly affectionate in front of other people. He's not a demonstrative person. I have a very warm son-in-law from a Jewish background, and they are all touchy and warm. And very slowly our family is learning. Then my second daughter married a Spanish Catholic from New Mexico, and he's the same way. So between our two sons-in-law, the old New England Puritan family is becoming more and more affectionate."

While learning to express affection, she continues to be fast,

Pictured (left to right) *are daughter-in-law Margaret, wife of son William Bell Chambers; William Bell Chambers; son Kenneth Carter Chambers; daughter Leslie Anne Chambers; the bride, daughter Lee Chambers-Schiller; son-in-law Lanning Schiller; Marjorie Bell Chambers; mother Katherine Bell; husband William Hyland Chambers; niece Laura Scanlan. When Dr. Chambers left the Colorado Women's College, a letter to the Denver* Post *editor stated that Marjorie "gave meaning to the term 'role model' and was [for C.W.C. students] the best example around."*

sharp, clever. "I've always used my intuition as well as my analytical ability. I think in that way I'm way ahead of both men and women. I've been a very creative person. But at the same time my father trained me to be analytical and theoretical. I've got the best of both worlds. I have used both sides of my brain. And I think, frankly, that puts me way ahead of a lot of people. I'm always outguessing them. I know where they are before they've gotten there themselves. Sometimes I will say, 'Well, what you are really trying to say is this.' And, they'll look at me, and say, 'You're right, how did you know?' I read body language, I read subtleties, and I read undercurrents." Womanly attributes. "Yeah. But at the same time, I can be very masculine and analytical," and precise, with a memory for dates, happenings. "But I don't know any phone number off hand. I don't want to clog up my mind with that kind of thing."

There is clearly a great deal in that galloping brain. The sinewy woman is an avid skier, swimmer, artist, pianist. And daughter Leslie adds, "She's a *fast* driver! If you ask for one word to describe her it would be 'incredible.'"

Marge's daughters take after her, says Bill. "They have similar interests, similar abilities." When asked if his wife was good-looking, he looks at his guest strangely—how could anyone not know of her beauty?—gets up and walks over to a self-portrait oil of Marge. "She is feminine, and surprises people because she is also a feminist, was a feminist long before it was popular. It's very possible to be a feminist and be a feminine woman."

In gloves.

How Marjorie Bell Chambers Did It

1. Marjorie Bell Chambers earned a bachelor's degree prior to marriage, and an MA degree while pregnant with her first child. She then raised her family.

2. The mother of four young children kept her foot in the career door by keeping well versed—through reading—in her chosen field of history while raising her offspring.

3. Her volunteer involvement in the Girl Scouts, the League of Women Voters, and, in particular, the American Association of University Women added both intellectual growth and administrative experience to her scholarly credentials and, again, kept her in touch with her history discipline.

4. As her children grew older, she, at forty-two, was hired on a part-time basis for the AEC as an historian and used the resultant historical document she created as a doctoral dissertation.

5. When Marjorie had difficulty handling household chores in addition to career obligations, she spoke with her family; they agreed to assume the majority of the homemaking responsibilities.

6. Chambers commands respect, the result of a self-confidence and assuredness nurtured by her years of important, prestigious volunteer—and later, paid—positions.

4

Bronze in Bloom

People are often unaware of their artistic talent. Gita Packer, sculptor, certainly was. Born in Jones County, near Abilene, Texas, in 1922, the young "country bumpkin" (as her grown daughter describes her) attended college, then fulfilled her childhood dream: she became a newspaper reporter. A few years later, she married, had a son, Craigie, Jr., and was pregnant again when several people close to her died tragically, including her father, who was critically wounded shortly before Gita's second baby was born. The new mother mentally collapsed and was institutionalized. After shock and insulin treatments, she returned home to raise Craigie and the baby, Julie, who years later as a preteenager ran away, beginning a ten-year self-destructive odyssey.

And Gita, never able to continue her planned free-lance writing because of memory lapses, turned instead to sculpture. When she was fifty.

"I had no idea I could do this," says Gita, musing about her art as she strokes a small bronze baby. "And I just learned to sketch the year before last!" But she feels it wouldn't have mattered if her talent was discovered when she was a child, for the young Julia Gita Bumpass, the oldest child with two younger brothers, "knew what I was going to do. I was going to be a newspaper reporter. We lived in the country, fifteen miles from one town and twenty-five miles from another, and the only thing we had was the rural mailman, who brought us the newspaper, and from time one, that, to me, was all there was in the world." Living on her mother's family's cotton and wheat farmland with sheep (later to be her sculpturing subjects), she attended a country school. "And we didn't have art classes." She began her education, at the fourth-grade level, where busing was available, for her family, poor, had no car to transport her. "Then, after high school, I went to Hardin-Simmons University in Abilene," graduating in 1943.

The tall, fast-talking college graduate recalls that in 1943 "the men went away to war and there were job openings for journalism majors." She obtained a position on the Abilene *Reporter-News* staff, where she worked for over three years, reporting and learning to use a big Speedgraphic camera when the *Reporter-News* photographer was drafted. "That was a wonderful time with those wonderful soldiers, you couldn't walk for them" in the military-base town. "We had dates running out of our ears. There was a shortage of everything except men."

"I loved it," but she and her roommate "wanted to go out into the world" and thought a job with the Galveston, Texas, paper would be spectacular. "Wow! But it was a terrible newspaper. And I had *really* always wanted to work with the Fort Worth *Star-Telegram.* That was my big thing."

She managed to obtain her goal, moving to Fort Worth in 1946 to write an amusements column. "I felt it was an accomplishment to speak with someone like Jimmy Stewart, Gregory Peck. I was impressed by successful people; I savored them. I seldom criticized. I admired what they did.

"And then I got married and then I got pregnant." The no-nonsense woman met her Cesar Romero look-alike husband, Craigie Packer—called Pack—in 1949 in a strip joint she was covering for the newspaper. Pack, an osteopathic physician who looks fifteen years younger than his sixty-eight, is ten years older than Gita.

When Gita became pregnant, she quit her reporting job. "Al-

Years after she interviewed numerous public personalities, such as Michael O'Shea (above) and Jimmy Stewart, Gita explains, "I need recognition."

though I thought I would someday stop working to have a child, that time hadn't come." The pregnancy was not planned. "But I was going to have children someday. I *was* getting a little fed up with work." She stayed at home with her infant son and wrote free-lance articles; then she became pregnant a second time.

"My father died the day before Julie was born." It was November of 1955. The circumstances of his shotgun death were unclear, and "a friend had just taken rat poison and died. Another friend's wife killed herself, and we found her body. . . . We chalked up eight in a year's time. You just can take so much. So when Julie was born, I went away—commonly known as having a nervous breakdown." When her father died "he was at the end of his rope," because of corporation speculation and manipulation of tangled oil rights on his Texas land. Gita, too, was unable to handle further disasters in addition to post partum depression: "Within six weeks, I was nobody." Completely dependent on an institution, "I had very severe shock treatments; they did it differently in those days." It partially destroyed her memory.

During the three and a half months she was institutionalized, "my mother took care of Julie and my son, who was five. And the dog." Pack stayed in Fort Worth, maintaining his practice and supporting the family. "Oh he's the *Rock* of Gibraltar."

Gita was home again for about four weeks, Craigie came home, then, later, baby Julie. Gita was frequently depressed and would cry. "It was all too much. But I had a maid then, and that helped." Pack, off on Mondays and every other Sunday and not beginning work on any day until noon, was not regularly helpful. "Not always, no. He's not very maternal." Her nervous laugh is somewhat disconcerting. She continues quickly: "After all that, it is very hard to pull your life together. I had no connections with what I was doing. As a matter of fact, the things closest to you are the things you completely forget. It's not unhappy things, it's not anything. It's random." The memory does not necessarily come back. "Not totally. Never." And you lose the ability to remember new things. "It's really hard. You've got to write notes." Craigie, an extremely active child, was in kindergarten and "I couldn't remember who the people involved with the kindergarten were.

"I did not go back to writing at all. I couldn't finish writing what I had started" because she would forget the beginning. "It was just a lost cause. One, I couldn't, and the other reason was that I didn't have time with two little kids." But as Gita stabilized and found her homemaking and mothering responsibilities easier to cope with, "I had to do *something*. I had always sewn and I've always made cookies."

Her husband, Pack, concurs: *"Always* doing things. Is she energetic? *Haah!* Doesn't sit still. Wonders why she gets tired. It's this nervous energy bit, and drive." He speaks slowly, noticeably in contrast with Gita's cynical, wisecracking style. You can almost feel her impatience to speak as he drones along. He laughs: "She has the ability to finish sentences." They compliment each other as he, less peppy and as clever, says: "We'd be bruised all over" if they weren't opposites. Gita connects herself with the commercial: "We are driven."

While the children were young, "I really had some kind of a dumb idea that you ought to hang around and make like a mother"; she did not consider finding a job. Pressed on this subject, she says seriously, "I couldn't have stood not knowing where the children were after school, that kind of thing." Motherhood: "That was my profession."

"And I played doctor's wife." One of a group of thirty closely knit osteopath couples, "We knew everybody and what they were doing, and what they ought to be doing." As a member of the osteopathics' association auxiliary, she was active in their medical school and hospital-related activities, and helped her husband in his office.

It was when her son was in the Cub Scouts in 1959 and had a project with clay that she began to see she might have artistic ability: "I played with the clay. It was great fun. And I knew about this sculpture class at the art center and had said, 'Someday I'll

Gita Packer, doctor's wife and mother.

take it.' " She decided 'Now is the time.' Although her parents were not artistic, her grandmother, a painter, "belonged to the school that copied, and I had always had the ability to duplicate something. Make a cake like another cake, make a dress that looked like another dress. And I was thrilled when my first head [in the portraiture sculpture class] looked like the head sitting there."

Next she ordered a kit that included sculpturing tools and a special wax which, when sculptured, was then sent back to the company for bronzing. "It was such fun that I did several little things."

She then found a local foundry—listed in the Yellow Pages— that charged $50 to cast her wax figures. She created the figure, and the foundry made a ceramic shell into which the bronze is poured, replacing the wax. She particularly liked working with wax because "you know that if you make a mistake, all you have to do is mash it down and start over. It's not life or death." After casting, she brought out highlights with steel wool, then rubbed the figures with floor wax. "I worked from photographs." She began to create animals she had photographed during the years in which the Packers had taken their children to the zoo, and on weekend trips where Gita, utilizing her newspaper experience, took pictures. "Animals are fun. There's always been an underlying interest in that." She also sculptured neighbors' busts but found that the models tended to evaluate her work and "I did not like the criticism thing." So she stuck mainly with animals rather than human beings: "Then I could do it on my own. Now I don't let anyone tell me anything. I decided that I should be doing this for *me*. It had to be something like writing or art for the sort of person I am. Something that belongs only to me. I'm just reporting on something in a different dimension now.

"I find it just the most wonderful escape," she continues. "I like sitting here, doing this alone. It's a great tranquilizer and a

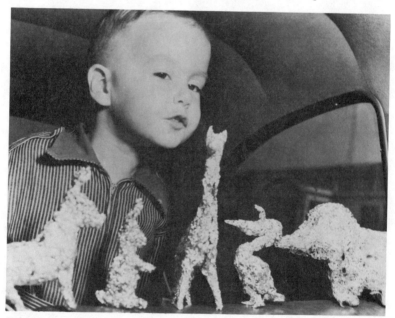

Baby Craigie, with aluminum foil toys made by Gita.

source of pride. It's the greatest thing I can do. It's so rewarding to see something happen, to see a face appear on a deer or a person." It is pleasurable to handle Gita's creations. "That's what they have all over painting. You can hold them, you can drop them—it will break your foot!—but they can be repaired and there's no indication that they've been damaged." At art shows, she displays a sign stating "Please touch."

"I was really hooked on it, so I had to find a way to sell them." Bronze castings are costly. If she could sell several to cover expenses, Gita could then keep one for herself. She speaks of "the frustration of getting rid of them, and that I don't like," because, again, she becomes vulnerable to criticism. "I don't like to be rejected. I don't like to meet someone who doesn't like them. It doesn't bother me all *that* much, but those are the bad things about it. But you can't crush me totally." Pack, interested in geology, cut and polished rock faces for Gita to use as bases for mounting her bronzes, making them more salable.

"Elsie Pease helped me very much." It was Elsie, another osteopath's wife, who "came and cooked dinner for us when we brought my mother home after my father had died. She's a friend. . . . Elsie put some in her antique shop. They were cheap then, because I was feeling my way. The first sale was a big thing; it's like your first job." Elsie (whose husband, a great fan of Gita's art, buys one of each Gita Packer miniature series created) also sold Gita's bronzes at antique shows. But Gita recognized she had to promote herself actively, and, says her husband, "she had to grit her teeth to get into it." Gita found other interested galleries and shows, wrote letters, called and traveled. It was 1974 and, "Yes," she says, "I pushed. I was accepted and rejected. Some sold and some didn't. And little by little . . . It's scary, putting yourself on the line, and being able to survive if knocked down." Pack went to art shows with her. "He'll stand by me, and if I fall over, he'll pick me up," although he does not aggressively promote her. Pack recalls: "She was quite fearful to go out and do a show. And she doesn't relish it now. But two years ago she would never have considered traveling to shows,

Pack, in their Fort Worth home.

as she does today. She sighs a big sigh of relief when it's over, although she'll be glad that she did it. And she feels that she can meet the next show better."

Although she must force herself to exhibit, the creative aspect is pure pleasure. Gita: "I enjoy doing something that I don't have to do," an advantage wives financially supported by a husband often have. Gita's husband admires both her work and its effects: "It is therapeutic," and he is intrigued by her ability to do several things at once. She "may be working on an animal in wax but she's mentally working on another project or two." Gita Packer epitomizes the thought that while a man might need a quiet corner to concentrate in, a woman is adaptable to working around distractions. The sculptor has her grandchild during the

DUAL LONGHORNS
3½x9

THE SMALL
BRONZES OF
GITA PACKER

DUAL LONGHORNS, limit 15
Other editions: 25

SANDHILLS
4½x4

Early on, Packer had business cards and brochures printed. And while the business of promotion worried her, she finally adjusted. "How can you be afraid of anything when you've sent your daughter off to Hippieville and your son to Africa?" Bottom: A Packer magazine advertisement.

day and overnight two nights a week and still manages to work. "Do I create when I'm calm? No, I create when there's an empty day." She grabs the time available. "I don't have to have an inspiration. I have to have an empty day! I just don't have that many."

The artist did find the time to take painting and drawing lessons recently, but "I was afraid that if I joined a class to paint or draw, I couldn't do anything. And I don't like failure. So I had some private lessons. And after we decided I could actually bend a line and draw," she began to sketch. Pen and ink. Pencil, scratch work. Then oils, mostly of animals. "I could really be hooked on drawing. It's portable and it's great. But I have to have a subject. I just can't reach up and create." She points to a wall full of paintings, prints, and drawings. Hers, her grandmother's, and those of others she admires. A picture of the lions her son, an animal behaviorist in the Serengeti plain, studies is next to a framed portrait of Julie, her daughter.

Julie speaks of her mother: "I admire the fact that when my mother wants something she goes out and gets it. She didn't used to really do that as confidently. She's a great believer in the mind and what it can do." After years of psychologists, psychiatrists, and institutions, Julie lives in Fort Worth, not far from her parents, as she works at building her own life. Slowly thoughtful like her father, the unmarried mother of a toddler—Gita often sculptures the child—says her childhood and teenage difficulties "affected my mother. It's now part of her personality; it's part of what made her strong." Strong enough to overcome mental illness, heartbreak over her child, to finally work at becoming a professional sculptor.

Gita: "I truly thought I just wanted a little corner here to make my little thing and enjoy myself. But somehow, along the way, I decided to be the best, maybe anywhere. I really started thinking big." Her work reflects her attitude. "The biggest thing I wanted as a kid was to work at the *Star-Telegram*. Not the *New York Times*. So that's as big as I got. And

Packer sculptures have been compared to stop-action photography. "I like," says Gita, "to fool with the titles." She used to enter "twenty-five words or less" contests (and often won) when home with the children, and title-creating fulfills that need now. Above: *"Mammoth Assist"*; below: *"Baboons and Buffoons."*

when I started sculpting I thought small. But now I don't."

"There are times," says Julie, "when my mother has ups and downs, but most of the time she's optimistic. She has always been optimistic either for or about me, and *that* takes some optimism. She's had a lot to put up with—all the problems I had —yet she has never turned her back on me. . . . I feel very proud of her. I've been supportive. I would say that she is one of the sweetest people around. I love her as a mother, and I also love her as a person. And since my mind has been cleaned out . . . I'm able to say that I've gotten to know her as a full person. I had no bad feelings toward her, as she thought I did. My troubles had nothing to do with my mother, truthfully. It had to do with my own mind." Julie now lives a calm life relative to her earlier years, which coincided with Gita's finding her new career.

In 1973 her daughter's world was in chaos as Gita started to produce limited editions of no more than fifteen castings of each miniature, which presently sell for $150 to $1,275, mainly depending on size. With hundreds of sales in the past twelve months, Packer regularly exhibits at New York and international shows and galleries, often winning awards, commissions, and prizes throughout the country. Gita was selected by the Fiftieth Anniversary Committee of the Serengeti National Park to sculpture their commemorative.

A comparison of her first attempts and present works indicates the artistic growth she has experienced. Appraiser Elsie Pease, who promotes Packer bronzes worldwide, considers Gita to be enormously talented: "Oh certainly! Yes!" She recalls an art dealer asking the age of the sculptor of the bronzes. When told, he shook his head: "Isn't that a shame. She's going to be famous someday, and she will not live long enough to see her fame."

But Packer is not sorry her talent was discovered late in life. If she had been aware of it earlier, "I don't think I would have done anything differently. I just haven't had enough time to do all the

Gita works with wax near her orchid-filled greenhouse, creating anatomically accurate sculptures that have a charming simplicity. The nineteenth-century French would have called her an "animalier," a miniaturist portraying subjects naturally and realistically.

things I want to. I should like to live a couple hundred years.

"Everybody has a different definition of 'making it.' I like to see people come to an art show, pat my work, and say how pretty it is. That makes me feel real good."

Packer has not suffered from mental illness since her earlier episode. "I refused to let it happen again. It slipped up on me when I wasn't looking. I thought I was immune. But now I'm in charge of my own life. It's going to all work out." She has had despairing periods of her life, "but I don't like unhappy people. What do you do? You get up, try for tomorrow! I don't live in the past. We should all be that way, maybe. That's what I've learned, in order to bloom again, so to speak. You've got to have the attitude that goes with it, or you're not going to make it."

Gita's husband, who, says Gita, "is proud, too, when I make something," shakes his head as he thinks of his wife. "I just look at her with awe," he says quietly. "I'm overwhelmed when I think about her sometimes. I'm just lucky as hell."

How Gita Packer Did It

1. The bronze miniaturist raised a son, now a research biologist at the Serengeti Research Institute, and a daughter, Julie, a young working mother.

2. Having helped her Cub Scout son with an art project, she found herself delighted with clay modeling.

3. Gita signed up for a Fort Worth Museum Art Center School sculpture class that had intrigued her for years.

4. Although she realized that her friend Elsie Pease's efforts to promote the bronzes were helpful, Gita faced the fact that she

"I have no message. My animals are just there, doing what they probably are doing in real life—being themselves and a pleasure to man. Sometimes I make a child and, rarely, a 'people.' But there's always an animal connection.

"I used to strive just for a space to cling to. Now, I consider myself something of a space capsule, complete within myself and proud of it. Who knows, I may come back as a rainbow!"

must also personally work at selling her art. She made telephone calls, wrote letters, and traveled to galleries, introducing herself.

5. Packer had illustrated brochures and business cards printed, suggesting to the art world that they were dealing with a professional.

6. Gita, says Pack, still does not relish attending a show. But knowing it is necessary, she nonetheless does it.

7. Not waiting for a large block of time or inspiration, the sculptor works when she can. It would be easy to use "no time" or "no ideas" as an excuse. She does not.

8. Her husband emotionally supports her: "When I make something, Pack is proud of it too." Pack cut and polished rock and geode bases for the miniatures. He travels with her, stands beside her at exhibits.

9. Although she has become financially and artistically successful in less than ten years, Packer continues to train herself, delving into untried media and broadening her artistic scope.

10. At some point in her career, Gita decided she would be at the top of her field. She believes in herself, and her work mirrors this positive attitude. Says an acquaintance, "She's devoting herself to her art and it's all beautiful."

5

Glamour Guru

June Eliel, a sixty-year-old Englishwoman born in India, became at age forty-three sole wage earner for and only parent to her five children, as her husband walked out of their lives. "Sometimes a good boot is helpful," she says philosophically, as she bounces out of her simple garden apartment, shared with her adult son, Jeffrey, on her way to one of the most unusual women's-wear enterprises in California, perhaps in the country.

It's a warm sunny day in Southern California and Eliel, after coffee in bed with the Los Angeles *Times*, said goodbye to Jeffrey and is now driving along the quiet Pasadena roads in her burgundy Vega. As she passes the old Pasadena Courthouse, she comments on her adopted town, fringed with the San Gabriel Mountains, an old winter vacation spot for East Coast millionaires: " 'Poor' is what they call South Huntington Road, but there were still three-, four-, five-hundred-thousand-dollar houses down there. Most of the money is socked in here." Pasadena is conservative in contrast with San Marino—"to be honest, quite snobby"—where her shop, Scarpers Bazaar, is located. Both towns have wide, clean boulevards, globe street lights, and rose-filled gardens.

She stops at a Pasadena dressmaker's shop, explaining that at Scarpers Bazaar alteration fees are exactly what the dressmaker charges, no more. Eliel makes nothing extra. Just as she sees no immediate profit when she shops—for hours sometimes—for the shoes to complete a customer's outfit, the correct scarf, jewelry. "If you don't have the right accessories, the damn things die, they look like blah." So they are located, by the expert—all gratis.

"It comes home to roost," she says as a yawn crosses her face; she's just jetted in from her twice-a-year five-day Paris trip and has been constantly active since. She chatters in her rapid British public school accent, at times uttering a clipped indecipherable phrase: "The last buying trip to Europe was so hectic. . . ." She is pleased to be home in California, a state she adores. In comparison with New Yorkers, who "all look angry," she feels "people here aren't set in their ways, and I rather like that. They're going to try something, change something, and they have the courage to try, at least."

She enters her small, elegant shop, dusts the few surfaces, and glances at an unusual wall clock as she realigns a red dress displayed flush against the beige wall. Eliel crosses the plush beige carpeting to a large coffeepot and begins to fill it as the first customer enters.

But wait—the matronly-looking woman customer, impeccably dressed, instead of surveying clothing offerings, walks over to a formica bar and props herself on a high cushioned stool, as June takes a lower chair behind the high counter. The business day has begun.

What happens in this shop? There are only three visible dresses, two on one wall and one placed on top of a square table. A mirror, some plants, and "Scarpers Bazaar" written on the arched doorway. Soft background music playing and coffee bubbling. But no other displayed clothes.

An early-morning shopper, opening the glass door and peering in, actually does ask, "What kind of store is this?" June explains after the woman leaves that "We don't get too much off the street—it's word of mouth." It is located in a quiet area, and most visitors know exactly what goes on inside.

Like the young elementary school teacher, married to a wealthy businessman and soon to make a trip to New York City with her husband. She rushes in to find out what is worn on the East Coast. And June, cigarette in hand, tells her, like a guru down below the ladies who are perched on their high-backed stools.

The door again opens. A friend walks in, bringing twenty garden roses for the shop, followed by a younger woman, sent by her network-executive boss on behalf of his wife. Although June has left her guru seat, the background counter conversation continues:

"Heidi, you look so elegant!"

"You can't believe the trouble I'm having with my contractor! . . ."

"Laurie! I haven't seen you in ages!"

Abruptly one of the women, Alice, stops chatting and, carrying her coffee cup, strolls into the narrow hall at the back of the shop, which opens onto what June calls the ladies' locker room, consisting of a bench and two three-sided mirrors on opposite walls. According to June, who walks in to join Alice, "Here, everyone gives their opinion." June brings an outfit, with a $34 cotton blouse. A $600 silk dress awaits, to be modeled next. Most dresses range from $200 to $350.

But Alice does not ask the price, and no tag proclaims it. Eliel, who says "Alice is one of our most loyal friends," decrees these frocks are correct for the woman. No discussion. But, alas, when tried on, the silk gown is a disaster. Alice: "Oh, I love it. What do you think, June?" June: "Take it off. You look God-awful."

June Eliel, fashion expert, has come a long way from the little Indian town in the foothills of the Himalayas where she was born to an English mother and a British Army father who later raised and trained race horses, "one of the top owners and trainers in Calcutta." Born in 1921, June was one of six children and the first girl after three boys. Although the children were born in India, they lived in their grandmother's home in England until her death, when June was twelve. At that point they attended a Catholic boarding school where "we were very loved kids. I'll tell you one thing—it taught us to be very independent. We had so much fun! We were Empire brats. . . . You know, you appreciate your home a hell of a lot more. You don't fight with your mother so much."

With no air travel, they saw their parents every two or three years. Yet, "We're a very close family. There was no togetherness so we loved and respected each other.

"I grew up in a totally different time. Women weren't pushed into careers. My mother asked me once what I wanted to be when I grew up and I said, 'A lady who sat on a couch, read a good book, and ate chocolates.' My mother nearly slapped me! She was smart; she wanted us all to have a career."

After high school June attended a Paris finishing school when she was seventeen. The year was 1938 and the war tensions were building. She returned to England as World War II began.

It was during the war that June met American bomber pilot William Eliel. After the family moved to California, five children were born: "I have three boys and two girls," born in 1945, '48, '50, '52, and '55.

"In 1968 my marriage really came apart when I was forty-seven, but I had gone to work before then."

June Eliel obtained her background experience working at Bullock's, a California department store, "because I had to." Money was needed. Her husband's earnings were sporadic, so "I started as Christmas help—selling. I hated it." She found it boring. But she did it. "I had to," she says again. "If you were a woman of forty without college in those days . . . the fact that you raised a family and had run a household—no points." She said to herself, "Life's too short," and decided to quit, as she was offered a position—through the recommendation of a previous Bullock's employee—at Gene Burton's, a local retail shop.

There she ran the shoe department and "I watched Gene operate. I learned a lot." Gene was a "fantastic businessman, a brilliant man." At Burton's she met her future partner, co-worker Karen Max. She and Karen, twenty years younger, both went to work, after Burton's, at the Andover Shop, another boutique in San Marino. June, who can't remember the year, turns to her deaf, slightly palsied son and enunciates clearly so he can lip-read: "Jeffrey, when did I start?" He answers, 1970. Her smile is full of affection, "Jeffrey does wonderful things for me." An extremely private individual who dislikes being photographed, June hides her feelings and personality except when she is with the likable Jeffrey, who puts his arm around her, with a big smile. "My mom," he says not too clearly. She's managed to instill independence and a positive outlook in "Jeffer," as she calls him. "There will be no eventual responsibility for Jeffrey, when I'm gone." He can live alone; they are together out of convenience and love.

"I'm lucky; I had the children," when Bill walked out of their lives in 1968. Her brood kept her spirits up, were companions, she says. An unusual outlook for a divorcee, but clearly sensible. "And I never felt Jeffrey was any great hardship to bear."

But the children did require caring for. "I was working and I realized Mike [then thirteen] had to do something because he couldn't come home from school at one-thirty or two in the afternoon and sit around. So I made him go out for track. And I used to go to all his meets." Both she and her son became avid track fans.

A friend shakes her head about Eliel's ability to turn a problem into an advantage: "I've known June since she came from India. She raised five kids under very adverse conditions [June, walking in, pooh-poohs this view] but she has the ability to be successful at whatever she does. She's strong."

Strong, clear-thinking, and a decision maker. She and Karen became proficient at helping customers obtain "a look" through an Andover Shop tradition. On Saturday mornings the buyers showed new merchandise to the employees, explaining how it all went together. Eliel took it all in.

Soon she and Karen, together, were doing the buying. "It was nice because we bought with their money. Not ours. Any mistakes we made . . ." Slowly June and Karen made subtle changes in the shop's method of operation.

"It started as a legitimate business but we got a little tired with it. I think it was mostly the crunch of '72, with money being so short." Business fell off. June was bored and said to customers, "Bring in your clothes; we'll go over them with you." Or "If you can't bring your clothes in, we'll come to your house." "It was really fun," as the business grew into a personalized service. The bosses' reaction, according to Eliel: "Why, they were so delighted just to have some movement!" What gave her the idea to switch the business along these lines? "Are you going to sit there, twiddle your thumbs all day?" Not June Eliel.

Business improved, and one year, after working extremely hard through the holiday season, June and Karen looked forward to their January bonus. "We had been toying with the idea of starting our own business and our bosses threw us into a positive state of mind when January came around and: 'Oh Sweet Pea, you haven't seen the bottom line! What a bad year we've got.' " There was to be no bonus. Yet, soon after that their employers bought an expensive house, cars, traveled to Europe, and June recognized for the first time that no matter how well she did and how hard she tried, "The owners are the ones who make the money." At that time she was earning $650 to $700 a month: "But it wasn't enough. It wasn't enough."

First the women looked for a location: "We went up and down Huntington Avenue in the middle of the night sometimes. When you start to do something, you just do it—find the right place. It's a matter of making a decision, and that's one of the hardest things. You luck into things if you believe they're going to be okay." Eliel calls a situation where an individual recognizes an opportunity and is able to take advantage of it, luck.

It was about this time that Karen married an architect, who agreed to monetarily back their enterprise. "If Karen's husband hadn't been there? I'd have gone down to the Small Business Administration. If you have enough knowhow, they'll give you money. They're not going to give it to any nincompoop who comes along. They don't just *give* the money away. You have to prove you know what you're doing. And you prove it with the fact that you've worked in this business." They were told they would need at least $60,000 to begin, but only $13,000 was borrowed. "We had our built-in clientele. And we got a very good rental deal and did the interior decorating ourselves—we didn't hire anyone. I think too many people put too much money into decorating the shops up with this, that, and the other. And they spend too much time on advertising. You buy the clothes, you sell the clothes. Get them out the door. *Then* you do the bookwork and worry about everything else. But the foremost thing you do is *sell.* "

That part was relatively easy because "we didn't have to wait until someone walked in the doors; that was the difference. They all followed us from Burton's and the Andover Shop." At first they had about two hundred customers. "We have about five hundred now. We do a lot of out-of-state work too.

"People who come in here are very similar. They're the 'I wasn't born to wealth, and now I've got it, and by God, I'm going to keep it' type."

Clients—June never calls them customers—explain what draws them to Scarpers Bazaar and the owners' no-charge personalized fashion-evaluation counseling:

"Do you know June and Nancy pack our suitcases for us? When I go on vacation, everything I have in my suitcase is right, and I will wear it."

"June said to me, 'Hang on to that dress. It'll come back.' And it did!"

"It's never obvious when June doesn't like someone."

And June says, "Our clients might look frivolous on the outside, but [said somewhat defensively] ninety percent of them are workers. . . . We have a lot of professional women, PhDs. . . . We [also] have doctors' wives, lawyers' wives, older women. They travel a lot, their children are gone, and they're enjoying life. These are the marriages that have survived.

"Price? Some ask; most don't. We keep an eye on price when we buy, but what we look for is fabric and fit, and something you can wear. Some of the younger ones aren't wealthy, but we manage them.

"They won't wear kooky stuff—they're not interested in labels."

The "clients" continue to model outfits—chosen from a back room by June—and, occasionally, buy.

And talk. "June'll say to us, 'Try it on, let's play with it and have fun' [for an hour]. And then, if we *want* to buy something, she'll say, 'No. You're doubling up. You have your blue wool in your closet. You can't have this, you silly little stick!' And we'll say, 'I *love* this one—I want it.' But June won't let us have it."

June encourages the visiting; it creates an atmosphere.

"Have you seen Joy? June and Karen have really put her together."

[To June] "I don't have any white britches, do I?"

"June'll point out what's wrong: 'Look how it fits you. . . .' "

The talk jumps back and forth. Clients enter and depart. June, unruffled, smooths, soothes, controls. To a customer who has just been told she cannot buy something because of a previously agreed-upon husband-decreed spending ceiling: "Remember, your birthday is coming up." I.e.: When the husband comes in to buy his wife a gift, June will sell him the coveted garment. Amazingly, June knew when the client's birthday was. Customer's comment: "Oh, you're right. It is!"

June explains over lunch, "Sometimes the shop is full—half are here to shop and half to eat. We have a lot of younger wives whose husbands are sent out of town quite a bit. And if you're a younger woman and you're stuck at home with the kids, you can't really go to a bar and get away with it. A breath of fresh air, away from the children—it really helps. Oh it's a crazy crazy place."

The afternoon begins. The bell on the door begins to tinkle regularly. It's group therapy, a counseling service.

June, who abhors being photographed, looks years younger than sixty as she chats with a client during lunch.

"No, no. . . . Well, a little bit," concedes June.

An unusual clothing store, based on two women's fashion savvy and service.

"Generally both of us [she and Karen] are here every day; we will often go out in the evening or on our day off just to shop [to Beverly Hills or the Newport Beach area]. We buy most of their accessories, their shoes, their costume jewelry. We even advise their husbands on what they need for Christmas, that sort of thing. . . . Do they go with us to shop for accessories? No, they trust us completely. Everyone trusts us. We have all their Master Charge, Bank Americard numbers over here. Often we call up stores, have things charged and sent to them. . . . Have you ever looked in a woman's closet and seen four white shirts, with the price tags still on them? We go right through their wardrobe and clean it completely out. And shoes! You have no idea how they buy shoes! Stacked up three boxes high. Some women like a shoe so they buy it in every color. That's ridiculous. . . . We also have women who are coming out of college who are going into the professional world. They have no time to rummage and they need a professional woman's look."

The day is over and Eliel, driving home, analyzes her success: "Too many women go into this business thinking they know about clothes and they don't. They think all you do is buy the clothes and sell them. But it doesn't work that way. And so a lot of them go broke.

"I think a woman with enough background—and one who really likes it too, and likes clothes and understands fit and color and can deal with the public and enjoys them—can do what we did. You can't rush [the customer] and you don't push them and you don't tell our kind of clients that they look lovely in something unless they really do. Then they trust you and you don't have to worry about the bottom line."

Profit reflects sales, which are dependent on judicious buying. As buyers at the Andover Shop, the now-partners had the manufacturing contacts, yet a line of credit was essential in addition to their original up-front money. "How did we get credit originally? I asked for a D&B number and I got it." She called Dun and Bradstreet, requested a rating before buying: "They start you with a low rating and they reevaluate you. And the next thing you do is, you pay your bills. Not like some of the stores. We've got a very high D&B rating in New York." In Europe she puts sales "on a letter of credit, which the bank pays. And you don't just go to the market and think you're going to buy the things and they're going to come. They're not. Because if you're small, you get put at the bottom of the line and half the stuff will never arrive. But if they know you and they trust you, in Europe, you don't have to worry at all. On a letter of credit, which the bank pays, it's all in the hands of the bank. When the order comes through and it isn't complete according to the way it was written, then it isn't paid. So the manufacturers are more apt to be careful that way. But with a lot of French manufacturers whom we trust, when the order is ready to be shipped, we pay them a third of it, the stuff arrives and then thirty or sixty days later, we pay them the balance. They'd rather do it that way because they don't like to be held down by the bank.

"The first time you go [to Europe to buy], you're absolutely terrified, dealing in so many languages and currencies. . . . And importing into the States is not easy if you don't know what you're doing. You have to have a broker bring the stuff in. But it's cheaper for us to go to Paris and buy than in New York, and it's actually less of a hassle. New York is a very rough market." The smaller European manufacturers are happy to deal with the littler businesses from the United States, rather than the conglomerates and large department stores, who are slow in paying and can break a manufacturer. "If the merchandise does not arrive on the right day, after a manufacturer has put a great deal of money and time into manufacturing it, the large department store can cancel the total order."

So a small concern does have certain advantages. Scarpers Bazaar's profits reflect this, although June "really truly can't say how well we're doing. My son in New York [a Saks Fifth Avenue buyer] asked me that and I said, 'Bill, I don't have a clue.' Pretty soon we'll have to sit down and go over the figures for the year. We have a bookkeeper. . . . We are quite successful. And we're building it all the time." Karen and June both draw a salary, but not excessive. "We won't do that, because money has to go back into the business. But during the year, as you can see, we're working all day long and we don't have time to bother with that [thoughts of profits]. People who worry about the bottom line all the time spend too much time on the bottom line and not enough time selling the stuff and getting it out."

This business is a two-person enterprise and, according to a customer, "Karen and June are a good balance—they get along beautifully. You know, they work so closely together, they travel together, you'd think they'd be at each other's throats. But they both have good dispositions, and they know what they're doing." Another customer: "They complement each other. That's their success. There are few people who work together as closely and as hard as they do. They have the adrenaline to meet the crises. When a customer's falling apart, they get the shoes, have them dyed, they deliver the necklace."

"We have our ups and downs," says June. "But by and large, we do work very well together. Karen's forty and I'm sixty. We've been together for ten years. We've yelled at each other a couple of times," but neither ever considered ending the arrangement, which seems ideal.

The business, Jeffrey, and her other grown children keep June's time filled. Talking of a client's tennis game, she says, "As a matter of fact, I like to play tennis too but I haven't had a chance to for a long while."

Although this woman works incredibly long hours, she still manages to look fifteen years younger than she is. Or perhaps her young appearance and stamina are the result of satisfying hard labor. Whatever the case, Eliel is not looking for change.

". . . Of course I'd marry in a *minute* if I could find someone I liked well enough. And I would not give up my independence. I've seen too many women get divorced and the next thing, they're sitting in singles bars, and they're remarrying, and it's all poof!

"I have a job to do. And I have fun doing it. If you believe in yourself, why not just go and do it? This big scream about women's lib gives me a pain. I'm sorry. If you believe in yourself, why do you need Gloria Steinem yelling for you? I can do my own yelling, thank you." As for women with little self-esteem: "They're not helping them, they're just confusing them more, the poor ducks. . . .

"You can't change things overnight . . . and things *have* improved a lot, even in my lifetime. When I was first on my own, I couldn't get credit anywhere. I tried a couple of times, then I got bored and I thought, 'I don't really need it.' But now I can get credit anywhere I want it." Eliel expresses sympathy for women who seem to have trouble organizing their own self-blooming, but she honestly doesn't understand individuals who cannot, as she did, accomplish whatever they wish.

But perhaps the "boot" given her when she assumed total responsibility for her children had an effect. "No. I would have done something anyway. I had to do something. I couldn't have sat home after they were grown. It mightn't have been this, but it would have been something. I could never spend my days going to luncheons because I had a taste of that in the air force—it'd bore the socks off me. And PTA gives me a pain.

"If I didn't work, I don't know what I'd do. Thank God the world's changing enough that a woman can do whatever she wants to do."

How June Eliel Did It

1. She first brought up her five children, including a handicapped son, to be independent, self-motivated adults.

2. Working as a salesperson in a local department store, she obtained basic experience in retail sales. "Go to Bloomie's and learn your business over there; I think the training is super. But realize you won't run your business like a department store," says June.

3. Because she impressed a fellow employee—often a source of better positions—that individual recommended June to businessman Gene Burton, who offered June a better job.

4. "I watched Gene operate." Observing experts at work while being paid to do a job equals free executive training.

5. Before forming a partnership, June worked with Karen on a day-to-day basis within the women's-wear field.

6. A client says Eliel is heroic to have done what she did while having the responsibility of the children. Eliel feels it is unfortunate that she is special. Many women cannot pull their lives together and do something when they have to, for economic or personal reasons. But they should be able to. It's not something extraordinary, according to her.

7. When Andover Shop management explained clothes coordination, June says she took it all in. Again, a free on-job education, if one decides to concentrate and learn.

8. "It was nice because we bought with their money. Not ours. Any mistakes we made" were therefore not repeated when Scarper's Bazaar was in business.

9. The realization came to June that the big profits ultimately go to the owner, not the dedicated employee. She decided she wanted to take on the hard work involved in being the entrepreneur.

10. June "got a good rental deal," and she and Karen "did the interior decorating ourselves—we didn't hire anyone."

11. Credit: Eliel was able to borrow cash from a personal source who believed in the venture—Karen's husband—and kept decorating simple and rental costs to a minimum, allowing Scarpers Bazaar to capitalize at $13,000 rather than the $60,000 experts said they'd need.

12. June expresses a lack of concern about the bottom line. Financial analysts would argue with this tactic, but for Eliel, work time is too precious to spend analyzing. Instead she sells. And it works. But at the same time the organization of the business automatically keeps expenses at a minimum. There are only two partner-employees, who, in addition to buying and selling, vacuum, dust, ship, replace bulbs, scrub the bathroom. Alterations are on a free-lance basis (hence, there is one person less on the payroll, receiving benefits, etc.), and, amazingly, to quote June: "I've never advertised in my life—never."

6

Crocus

It is Saturday morning. The Florida legislative session in Tallahassee ended on Friday, and Representative Elaine Bloom flew to her Miami home that same night. In spite of her husband's efforts to keep her home on weekends, once again she has a Saturday obligation, this time at the University of Miami: State Representative Elaine Bloom will be a panelist in a "Crisis in Education Issues and Options" seminar.

Bloom, in a wraparound jersey knit dress that accentuates her waist, and carrying a full briefcase—in beautiful mahogony leather, a gift from her husband—is well-proportioned, petite, perfectly groomed. She smiles pleasantly at the audience as the moderator introduces her: ". . . hardly needs an introduction. Well known as the madame of education in the Dade [County] Delegation, presently in the House of Representatives from Dade County . . . considered by *Miami* magazine as among the women who have made it, cited for Excellence in the Community by the Dade County NOW organization, Citizen's Award for Manpower Planning Counsel . . . and a long list of activities. . . ."

Wearing a tiny gold gavel around her neck, Elaine stands. It is her turn to speak. Feminine, assertive, direct, with a soft, distinct voice, she begins to discuss her support of a high school graduation exam and her sponsorship of a bill in the Florida House that would require teachers—most of her audience—to take a competency test every five years. The group is hostile.

The cameras flash as Bloom begins to speak, gesturing with her hands. At the end she adds, "If you disagree with me violently, I hope you'll offer constructive suggestions."

A rebuttal unfolds. Bloom leans her chin on her hand and her head turns toward her opponent. An impenetrable expression masks her thoughts. A second speaker, representing Dade County's three thousand migrant workers, asks rhetorically: "Might this testing be biased?" Bloom begins taking notes with a felt-tipped pen. She passes a half wink to an acquaintance in the audience as another participant speaks of teacher responsibility.

The floor is open to discussion. Bloom is challenged; she hits back, swiftly, cleverly, and logically. Next, she apologizes in advance for tooting her own horn, then tells of the educational strides implemented at her instigation.

The moderator rises, wishing to intercede, but Bloom continues to hold the floor—with politeness and grace, but she holds it. The moderator sits down.

Elaine talks clearly, quickly, at an even pace, smoothly silencing someone with whom she no longer wishes to speak without conveying disapproval. Her husband gives his complimentary explanation: "Elaine makes everyone feel so important; she gives them an accolade in one form or another and does it so naturally that they can't help but feel good."

The panel meeting has been over for twenty minutes now, but the representative seems unable to work her way out of the room. People are lined up, waiting to speak with her: "Elaine, thank you for all you've done for teachers." A department of education official wants to set up a meeting. Another wishes to discuss the competency-test proposal: How will it affect this individual, a seasoned teacher who has been out of college for twenty-five years? Finally, though, the center of attention is out the door and soon on her way home.

Being the Miami representative at the state capital in Tallahassee is a new sort of experience for her, yet at another level it is

not. Elaine Berstein Bloom—from the time she was in school—
has been a leader.

She was born in New York and began attending Bronx High
School of Science when she was only thirteen. She graduated in
three years and then went on to Barnard College of Columbia
University, where she met Philip Bloom, a Columbia Law School
graduate, about to be appointed to the antitrust division of the
Department of Justice.

Philip remembers going to a dance, "And I met Elaine coming
in the door." She adds, "It was immediate electricity." They
married one year later, in 1955, when Elaine was eighteen. The
couple settled in Riverdale, New York, and Elaine was graduated
from Barnard the following year.

By 1961 Philip Bloom was an assistant New York State attorney
general. And Elaine, who as a college student was active in Jacob
Javits' first Senate campaign, now became involved in a mayoralty
race, and was working for a television station when her first child,
Anne, was born.

It was in 1962 that the Blooms moved to southeastern Florida.
And it was there that the twenty-five-year-old wife and mother
began to emulate her own mother, Ethel Berstein, who had been
continually involved with good works when Elaine was a child.

Elaine and her brother—older than her by five and a half years
—come from a talkative, lively household. Elaine describes her
father, a retired watchmaker, as "a hard-working man, a deep-
thinking person. I don't know anyone else who has read all the
volumes of the story of civilization by the Durants." Elaine's
mother, who never worked in a paid position, is, according to her
daughter, "Totally up to date, totally. She should be with the
State Department, and I'm not just joking. . . . She was always
vitally involved with major organizations. I grew up with the
feeling that if I stayed true to the tradition of marrying a nice
husband and having a nice family, the best thing I could hope to
do was to be a full-time volunteer."

Elaine, pregnant with her second child, expressed just this

notion at Barnard in 1959. She had been brought back to speak at a career day, asked to address herself to the possibilities open to the government major. "I said the highest good was to use your skills and your knowledge in the area of government to improve society as a whole through volunteer organizations."

Elaine herself utilized her college training in this manner, after her own graduation with a degree in government. "I was supposed to go to law school," she says, but volunteer roles appropriated her time. The Miami chapter of the National Council of Jewish Women, for one, "spent a lot of effort—and even money —on me," she recalls. The Council provided leadership training and, at one point, sent her to Vanderbilt University's graduate school of management.

Her husband remembers, "It was a step-by-step progression," as she threw herself into whatever she was doing, did it well, felt a sense of accomplishment, and went on to bigger things. She has talent, ability, confidence instilled in her by herself, he feels, and by him. "I show her appreciation. She likes to know she's done well, and I commend her."

Yet as her two children grew older and she became, in 1971, at the age of thirty-four, one of the youngest women in charge of the 2,800-member NCJW section in Miami, her husband thought she was being abused: "She would spend eight to ten hours a day with these groups and, to be direct, many organizations had paid employees who were using *her* to do their work. Phone calls all day, and at night . . ." Did he ever consider suggesting she stop working and stay home? "No. There was no sense in curbing her. It would have been unfair because she had so much talent." Elaine's daughter was a young teenager as her mother assumed the presidency, which, says Elaine, meant that "for all intents and purposes, I had a full-time job." Anne recalls her mother instilling in her—just as Ethel Berstein told a young Elaine—how vital this volunteer work was, for the recipients, for Elaine, and ultimately for her family. Anne says her mother "encouraged floundering women . . . and I've learned from that. I too want to help other people."

Elaine's steadily progressing involvement made her children more responsible for their own lives. And her daughter observed that "the more my mother did, the more self-assured she became." But Philip saw a flaw. "I told Elaine I thought it was about time to treat her skills as if she had a job, and go out and earn a living and get paid for what she was doing. She was accomplishing more than the people who were earning salaries."

"What happened was," Elaine recalls, "I was president of the Greater Miami Section of National Council. And when I was finished with that responsibility, my husband said to me, "You're a has-been at thirty-five unless you go out and professionalize what you've been doing.' It was his insistence that I find a paid-employment situation that got me to move out—and in fact I felt very very upset at that point. What would I ever do? Who would pay me for what I knew how to do? I didn't think I would be equal to the responsibility of tying into something that would in effect be paid professional employment."

When she first moved to Florida, seventeen years before, her hands would shake badly when she stood up to submit an oral committee report. "I was terribly, terribly nervous." But now: "Believe me, I had developed incredibly." Her nonpaying positions with charitable groups were responsible for her poised appearance.

She decided to let several contacts—made through her volunteer efforts—know she was looking for work. And to her surprise, she began to get telephone calls. From the Community Relations Board, from the University of Miami, and from a station wishing her to conduct a call-in radio show, "Women's Power Line," which she did for three years, sharing responsibilities with three other women. She began to recognize her worth.

In the living room of her house, leaning against a chair, is a tote bag that states A WOMAN'S PLACE IS IN THE HOUSE AND THE SENATE. Elaine Bloom took that message to heart. "I finally realized that all I had been doing did add up to time and experience needed

E. Bloom, Candidate, poses with family for her 1974 campaign brochure. Says daughter Anne (standing), "My mother is my best friend. That's probably a rare thing to feel."

for public office. But even funnier, I looked back at all the things that I had ever done, and it had all been a progression building up to a life in political activities. Look at me—a nice average housewife who did a lot of community service—I just turned it into something appropriate. The leaders of the PTAs and the Junior Leagues and all the other organizations are retired as presidents and there is really little else that is done with them. Yet the heads of the organizations like the Junior Chamber of Commerce or the United Fund—as males—are told, 'You did such a great job. Why don't we run you for the City Council? We really need you on the council commission.' *These* are people we propel into office.

"But I never looked at my experience from the standpoint that a male would look at it: What are my natural goals? . . . Yet I did

take advantage of the fact that I was a woman at the right time
—in the seventies. I like to think we are now going to take advantage of the new resource for public office: women."

When Elaine Bloom was asked by the *Miami Herald* in 1971 if
she would consider running for public office, she answered,
"Right now my children make demands of me, and they should."
And her daughter was quoted: "She's always here when we need
her." Three years later, however, Elaine felt it would be possible
to assume political office, including several months a year in
Tallahassee, and still be available to her husband and her children, now aged eleven and fifteen.

In 1974 Elaine Bloom ran against a six-year incumbent for a
state representative seat and won with over sixty percent of the
votes.

Bloom sees volunteer work as an excellent springboard into
politics, a training ground. "When you work with the Jewish
women's organizations, you keep on having to build a bridge
between people who think they're far apart. . . . You need to find a
common denominator." These are, she says, the same talents a
mother uses when she has two battling children. "I think they're
general tools that parents need. They are also management tools
and helpful in interpersonal relationships. . . . But we've never
identified these particular skills that women—mothers—possess."

One of Elaine's interests within the legislature is the family and
children. She continues to submit bills that will, in her mind,
constructively affect the family and marriage. The Tallahassee
Democrat's article "Dade Legislature Blooms in the House" spoke
of Elaine's particular interest in personal family responsibilities.

The Blooms' teenaged son, David, moved to Tallahassee with
his mother for the first three years Elaine was a Florida state
legislator. He's now living in the Miami area with his father. Their
daughter attends Yale. Elaine, who "moves quickly," according
to a friend, continues to be away from home four nights and five
days during the legislative sessions, plus meeting other obliga-

Elaine, formerly bazaar-organizer extraordinaire, is surrounded by supporters as she watches over her husband's shoulder as election returns arrive at her headquarters. Victory!

tions, including speech dates and campaigning, away from her family. "The first few times you try to write a menu for every day you are going to be away, and color-code the clothes. By the tenth time you say, 'I'll see you. There's food in the freezer.' "

"I don't know how she does all the things that she does," says David, shaking his head as he talks, "but she does." He sees his mother as an "intelligent, very organized" individual who takes care of the important things; she is, he says, with her present political career, "more available now than she was as a volunteer." He says she's a good mother and when asked if he likes her, responds: "I love her." Someday he will look for a woman like his mother to marry, "but I don't think there is anyone else like her." He again repeats that he doesn't know how she does it all; it surprises him that she can also be an excellent cook after working all day. "Whatever she puts her mind to, she does it right!"

She decided long ago that her most meaningful role is as a mother and wife. On her marriage: "In addition to being happy with our situation and with each other, I think we're happy with who we are."

An advantage Elaine has, as she builds a professional life, is a husband who delights in her achievements; he indicates his pride by hanging Elaine-connected documents on his office wall. A friend of the Blooms comments, "It's the best marriage I've ever seen."

But Philip does admit he wishes there had been more time for Elaine to spend with their two children, guiding them. Elaine mumbles about the quality of the time. "I don't go for that," he

Representative Bloom is hard at work in May of 1976.

says, pauses, then admits, "Now I could have done the same thing [spent more time with the children], but I justify it, rationalize it by saying I was busy working."

With prodding Philip admits—after some generalized complaining about often losing his weekend time with his wife—that "we have a better marriage because she's busy," although Anne says her father "still wants dinner on the table, he still wants clean clothes."

Which he gets, because the politician-mother-wife is constantly in action. Her multi-jobs, by necessity, overlap. As she talks about her professional career, Elaine putters around her kitchen, which she keeps kosher, her husband says, "100 percent all the way."

The phone rings five times while she is putting together some lunch. Nothing seems to faze Elaine, and she continues to display a cool, easygoing face. Anne says, "She is the calmest family

Elaine Bloom with Birch Bayh at a 1977 political gathering.

member, without doubt." This becomes obvious as an aide charges into the house (and Philip moves from the kitchen, even more chagrined that additional weekend time is being displaced) and sits at the kitchen table; Elaine continues to work at the counter, tossing cucumbers and tomatoes while weighing political strategies. Aide Donna Dupuy says her friend and boss is "the most selfless person I know in politics. No lip service. There is no jealousy when another woman succeeds. A lot of women feel, 'If it ain't me, I don't want it.' " Not Elaine. Dupuy explains that, while some individuals look at the salad, Elaine sees the anchovies and the radishes; she has terrific instincts. "Elaine's probably the most patient person I know. She never gets mad. I have seen her angry twice in two years," and the two women work in close contact. Philip, returning to the kitchen, agrees his wife is extremely even-tempered. Where does her anger go? He shrugs, "I don't think she's ever angry." Donna adds that she is always late, however. It is comforting to hear of one flaw.

Elaine recognizes her limitations and strong points: "I don't think of myself as a top-flight administrator but I do think of myself as a super legislator." Philip interjects his unbiased opinion: "She has a way of bringing diverse views and problems together, succinctly, stating them, summarizing them and then finding the solution. She's *excellent* that way. She's a staunch supporter of the ERA but she's not oppressive or abusive toward people who do not have the same view."

Philip's view of his wife is positive, on all levels. "Elaine always looks good to me," the extrovert says in an unexpectedly soft voice. Elaine laughs and adds, seriously, "My appearance is improving as I get older." Assurance coming through? Satisfaction? "She's always been a very attractive woman," says her husband, "and I agree she gets better-looking as she gets more mature." And more successful.

On the day of the University of Miami education panel meeting, Elaine Bloom was walking along a sun-bathed path when she encountered University of Miami President Henry King Stanford. They greeted each other warmly and Elaine explained she was

Philip and Elaine Bloom flanking the author at a 1979 Miami press gathering.

going to be included in a book about Late Bloomers. President Stanford smiled and said: "Call her a crocus because she blooms in the snow."

How Elaine Bloom Did It

1. Elaine obtained a college degree, married a man who admired her abilities, and had two children.

2. Following her mother's example, Elaine involved herself in women's volunteer activities, eventually receiving formal executive training as well as practical managerial experience.

3. From a trembling volunteer concerned about giving an oral committee report, Bloom evolved into a confident, articulate spokeswoman. Elaine developed, according to her daugher, "an enormous capacity to express herself *and* to listen to others."

4. Urged by Philip to view her years of personally rewarding but unpaid labor as significant professional skills, she searched for related job possibilities.

5. Bloom saw that a public avocation is a natural progression from a volunteer position and decided to run for political office.

6. Elaine Bloom joined together and developed her areas of expertise and interest. Her concern for the quality of life for the individual and for the betterment of her community and the world through volunteer endeavors and, later, political action combined for an exciting career.

7. Epitomizing the concept that a late-blooming career is particularly rewarding when it strengthens an already solid family life and marriage, Elaine and her husband, Philip, together work toward Elaine's continuing political success. Her daughter says, "The more she's done, the more self-assured she's become. What happened to my mother was good for all of us."

7

Not Right

"I had no *idea* I'd ever be in broadcasting, and certainly not to this degree." The wrinkle-free face of radio personality and Public Affairs Director of Baltimore's WWIN, a black-oriented disco-rock station, belies her forty-some years of age. Mary Matthews Clayburn—Maryland listeners know her as Mary Cee —a charismatic, successful black woman, started life with few material possessions. But the ingredients necessary to build her strong character, personal ambition, and assuredness were there, in her South Baltimore home: "When you are deprived of certain things yet have a strong family with all of your basic emotional needs met on a constant basis, there's no way to know you're poor."

The radio and television personality's father, James Matthews, was a Baptist minister; his wife Eleanor, eighteen years younger, was one of a farming family of fourteen, and "was the girl who was left home to care for the parents as they got older," in Madison County, Virginia. "And my father and his younger brother ran away from home in a boxcar when they were very young. As a boy, he remembered looking up at the sky and saying to himself, 'There's so much more to this world than what I see, and I'm going to find it some day.'"

The young dreamer educated himself in Baltimore; he read and attended night school, earning his high school diploma. He was well versed in the Bible, and his English, handwriting, and spelling were excellent.

Matthews was forty-seven when Mary was born in 1933; his daughter remembers, "I sometimes asked him, 'Are you sure you're not my Grandpa?' . . . I am the second oldest. My older sister, who married when she was seventeen—her husband was seventeen too—went back to school after her seventh child was in college" and obtained her bachelor's degree, then a master's degree. Her younger sister, a college graduate, works for Baltimore's Pratt Library. "My brother, Flip, is dead." While he was in the service and away from home, their mother passed away, and, according to Mary, "Flip never fully recovered from my mother's death. They had been just inseparable. . . . He refused to believe she had died. . . . It was a great shock to him when he actually saw her in repose." A year after his service discharge "he started seeing a woman old enough to be his mother. A year later, he killed her and himself." Fully clothed, they were peacefully sitting on a bed together, feet on the floor but resting back. "His service revolver—he was a policeman—was in his hand."

The tightly knit family held themselves together through this tragedy because, to the Clayburns, the family unit was the important relationship. "My sisters and my brother had a kinship that you wouldn't believe—what we did for each other! We realized early in life that if we stuck together we could accomplish what we wanted. My father was very strict. No parties. No dancing, no this, that, or the other. But we did it *all* and he never knew. We'd help one another get dressed, and lower each other out the window. We knew when he was home; he always put his hat in one place. And we worked around it. It wouldn't be uncommon for one of my sisters to say, 'I'm going out tonight. You stay up and let me in,' because at a certain time my father was going to lock the door; *presumably* everybody was in.

"It wasn't easy, but we outfoxed him! It was part of a game. . . . Flip, my brother, was very good at baseball. My father said, 'You will not play baseball on Sundays.' Yet he pitched for the team! It took all of us to get him to those games." Dressed in a suit and tie, he would pass his father's study at the church, then rush to the car where his sisters dressed him in his baseball uniform and then raced over to the ball park. Picking him up when the game was over, they redressed him in his church clothes in time for him to be home when his father arrived.

She smiles, then becomes sober: "My father was a minister all of my life, and I saw him go through traumatic things most people would fall under. When you see that kind of strength demonstrated day after day after day, it's got to rub off on you."

There is a pause. Rock music is playing in the background as Clayburn, sitting in her radio station office, glances to the right

TV and radio personality Mary Cee, in 1979.

at a small sign: THE CROSS IS IN MY POCKET. A religious woman, she often goes to church—"I enjoy it; you need to be nurtured spiritually. It gives you feelings." She brings religion to the rock station's listeners through her Sunday gospel program. "Religion is to be lived. My strong religious background keeps me in a path." She often thinks, "My father would die if he knew this" or, "What would my mother think?"

Her mother, who was always waiting for her father at night after church, in the background, was "an extremely righteous person, very quiet. People probably thought she never had an independent thought in her life. She was a *good* person." Mary remembers her mother saying to her spouse: "But it isn't right to do that. . . . It isn't fair." Mary Clayburn tilts her head to one side and reflects. "But never in front of anyone. I never heard her say 'not right' to him in front of anyone. She built an image of respect around him.

"My father impacted upon our lives more than my mother, who was *extremely* sheltered and *very* naïve." Perhaps Mary's character is imbued with more of her mother's personality than she realizes. As the public voice of Baltimore's WWIN, as a commentator and interviewer, Mary Clayburn, according to her boss at WWIN, consistently stands up and states what she feels to be fair. Instrumental in decisions made by city and state political figures, she has received a commendation from the mayor. She speaks of "doing and saying what I think is right, even when I have to stand by myself, when it isn't popular to say certain things. Every day black youngsters are being influenced by what they see on TV and hear on the radio and what is going on in the community. And when people live with little hope all the time, wrong can look so right. It's not easy to convince these young people that they're making problems for themselves later in life." When looting took place during a severe Baltimore snowstorm, Mary spoke up, according to friend and fellow employee Susie Wood: "If Mary sees something must be said, she doesn't bite her tongue." On the air and in the press, Mary explained to the black community that the

destruction and theft ruined, for example, a neighborhood drug-
store, and older people no longer had an accessible supply of
necessary medication.

"If I think a program is good and blacks aren't in it," she writes
a letter. "And I get after people for not coming to us and offering
the kind of programs to black audiences that they're offering
elsewhere." When Clayburn has reviewed educational films produced by charitable groups, "I've pointed out, 'You don't have
any blacks in this.' " When a health organization warns that
blacks in particular die of high blood pressure, Clayburn suggests
a more positive message: "Do specific things to take care of
yourself, and live."

And her advice is taken. The Cancer Society planned to conduct Pap smear testing in a mobile unit; "You can do high-blood-
pressure screening on a truck, or TB screening, but not a Pap
smear. Set up a center, do it in a hospital where people can dress
and undress in dignity," says Mary who, when consulted, asked,
"Are you going to white communities with this?" The American
Cancer Society listened to Clayburn. "Sure! They were well-
meaning, but they just hadn't thought. You can't take away people's dignity."

Mary Matthews Clayburn knows about dignity and pride. And
about pain—emotional and physical.

"I had been sick all of my life. It wasn't until I was sixteen that
we were sure that it was sickle-cell anemia." Mary is a captivating
storyteller, her eyes sparkle, and as she relates a family situation,
she will often say, "Does that make sense?" "Do you think so?"
"What do you think?"—drawing her listener into her story. But
the smile softens as she recalls the unpleasant part of her childhood, the illness. When she was small, her disease was thought
to be leukemia, rheumatic fever, or heart murmur—"which I do
have now because of the sickle-cell anemia. I was in high school
when it was diagnosed properly. All my sisters say I was my
father's favorite; I think I was," but, perhaps, "because I was
sickly I required a lot of attention. I remember nights when my

parents would rub my arms and legs all night, taking turns. Ah, the pain was terrible. And the rubbing was anesthetizing, to the point where I couldn't move. I would go to sleep hearing their voices in the background." No one knew what was wrong with her, "and nobody much cared, because you're black. This doesn't happen to anybody else. So it just wasn't that important." Her gym teachers—"who, instead of allowing me to sit down, would make me 'suit up' and stand in the corner, barefoot: 'If you can't take gym, you stand there and watch everybody else.' It was a punishment." But this has changed. "Oh Lord, yes. They don't do that now. Some days I could take gym and some days I couldn't. It depended upon how I felt. But nobody understood this."

The disease—in its worst form, fatal—is debilitating, and the five-foot-tall, 119-pound woman learned that weariness and dampness could precipitate severe joint pain and a crisis. As Mary understood her limitations, she learned to live with them. "My crises were not as frequent as my youngest sister's," who also has the genetic disease. "I wasn't out of work as much partly because my frame of mind about my sickness, about myself, was different. I was beginning to be pleased with myself, and no matter what illness you have, you can make it a little bit worse or you can make it a little bit better. I just learned how to care for myself" while a high school student.

She did not think about her future when she was a teenager. "There weren't too many plans at that time. I came out of high school in 1952, and there were not many opportunities for black women unless they wanted to be a secretary. And that was a big thing in the black community. I remember how proud my mother was when I got my first clerical job."

She attended an all-black high school where a black class system was perpetuated. A girl who was fair, with perhaps a professional father, was "in" and, "I guess every dark-skinned black girl my age, then, wished that she could be somebody else. You were not accepted into black sororities if you were dark-skinned"—

unless you had a special parent. "It was part of the black culture. There were black adults who did this to children, teachers who crushed a lot of black women during those fifties. It was particularly damaging to me. But I did overcome it because I had my mother and father saying to me, 'You're just as good as anybody.' " With integration, this psychologically stifling class system ended. "With all the interracial problems they have in the schools today, they are way ahead of those things. Kids can now make it—you *can* push above the crowd, if you really want to. It doesn't matter what you look like." The afro Mary wears today was "unheard of" in the fifties. "To make my hair as much like yours was the thing in high school, and God help the girls who couldn't do it. It's changed a lot. My sons laugh when I tell them about all this."

But "these things existed" in the three Baltimore black secondary schools, as Mary graduated and obtained her first clerical job and thought about a husband. "Then all girls thought about getting married. I had dated a guy for seven years. I thought he would be the one. But he went into the service and when he came out, he had changed, I had changed, and that was that."

She attended Baltimore Junior College as she began working for the Pratt Library System, which had some thirty branch libraries in the greater Baltimore area, and "the bus would pass these beautiful houses on my way to work and I remember looking out of the windows at the homes. That's when I began to see that other people had other things. When you get older and you go uptown, you see what you don't have. But truthfully I didn't know this when I was growing up."

Her experiences within the library enabled her to see that there was a larger world beyond her small black society. She first worked in a predominantly Polish-American community, and "dealing with racism is a curious kind of thing. You get children who have been told certain things at home about black people, coming into the library without their parents, and *you're* the authority and they're dealing with you, one to one. I've had them say, 'Can I touch your skin?' To see if any of this is going to come off. And you bend down to write, and you feel the little hand touching your hair." She grew to love these children. "Many of them discounted what their parents told them because of their relationship with me."

And when she was transferred to the Rolling Park section of Baltimore, a wealthy predominantly Jewish community: "You see how people with money live. And I guess I learned that it is true: They're the easiest people to deal with. They had class." Were they simply better at hiding their feelings? "Maybe that's it. But if it kept me from being hurt, more power to them." Mary tilts her head again and considers. No, she thinks these people were good individuals. "They looked at me as a person. It's not so hard to tell. Even my dog knows who likes him and who doesn't." Her dog flaps his tail as his mistress looks at him.

Mary eventually worked within the black community while employed at the library, in all neighborhoods and on the bookmobile: "I learned to work with people. I liked everything I ever did at the Pratt Library. It put me in touch with so many different kinds of people." Her coworkers, including many foreign scholars, were "a cut above the average individual. Everybody at the library reads. It's all around you. I hated books when I was in high school, yet now I love to read. And, if it's in print, I can find it" —a help in her media career, years later.

Mary lived with her parents while at the Pratt Free Library "until I got married, at twenty-three." She was working at the library when she met Mack, her husband-to-be. They fell in love and "he bought me a ring. I showed it to my mother and my father. My father made me give it back. I was *twenty-three!* He said 'Who does he think he is?' " Mack hadn't asked the Reverend Matthews for Mary's hand. "My father was just old-fashioned."

Mary muses on her father's reaction to Mack as a potential husband. "I don't think he really ever wanted me to marry Mack. We had different upbringings, different values. My father didn't believe it would work." Mary explains that her spouse—"very talented, a tremendous head"—was an only child whose needs were totally met by his mother and his aunt; he never learned to share.

Mack, a high school graduate with some college credits, had been in the service, and after their 1959 marriage, the ex-master sergeant worked for the postal system. Mary continued at the library, where, by the age of twenty-six, she was secretary to the head of the history department and supervisor of the clerical workers. Then "I went into a research department at the Core Library" until becoming pregnant with her first child.

"I thoroughly enjoyed being pregnant, a whole new experience. Only I didn't realize sickle-cell anemia could come back in another form." Now she had difficulty breathing and pains in her sides as she entered the hospital a month before delivery. The physicians were puzzled. Sickle-cell anemia was not on the maternity patient checklist: "Everything else you can think of. But not sickle-cell anemia. And I didn't think to tell my doctor I was a sickler. And he never thought to ask." Finally the connection was made. "Everything was experimental for me"; she required surgery to control eye hemorrhages.

"I didn't have trouble with the delivery," and, after Mark's birth, Mary worked part time at the library when her husband was home to care for the baby. When she became pregnant with her second child, she was cared for by a hematologist as well as a gynecologist. It was not until her second child was born that a pattern was recognized. "The sequences of eye operations I had —four with the first pregnancy, four with the second pregnancy —helped the doctors to understand that the chemical changes of pregnancy caused the disruption."

Her second child, Myron, was a toddler when she decided to work again. "I had a babysitter across the street." Her older child, Mark, was at a neighborhood nursery school, and Mack, who started work at 6:00 a.m., was home by 1:00, when "he would pick Mark up at the nursery school, go home, and start the dinner for us." After her many years working at the library she considered her options and decided "it might be interesting to do something else."

Radio station WEBB was in the neighborhood. Mary walked in and spoke to them about a clerical position, and they, surprisingly, said, "We're thinking of putting a woman on the air. Would you like to audition?" Friend Susie Wood says Mary recognizes an opportunity and will use it to her best advantage. She did just that: "I have a heavy voice. In school I was so ashamed of it. I talked under my breath to hide it. My voice was always a negative. I just turned it around. When I got into broadcasting . . . boom! I let it all out." Accepting the job on a trial basis, she was worried about the console disk jockeys operate. "You have pots, spot master, mikes. You don't have time to think. It has to be automatic. So I made a huge diagram of the console, took it home, placed it on the kitchen table. I pasted these little knobs on, turning the mike switch, buttons. I made myself a mike, hanging down. Did a whole show on my kitchen table." She was to do a 5:00 a.m. Sunday morning gospel show, appropriately. "My father *was* a minister." She remembers saying once, when she made a mistake, "Who's listening anyway?" The phone rang immediately. "From then on I did the show as if someone was listening."

Soon Mary was creating jobs within her job. "I started hawking on the radio for SCA [sickle-cell anemia] in 1968, when I was first in broadcasting." As she brought the problems of SCA to the public's attention, a newspaper columnist interviewed her. Then, "I got a few friends together and said, 'Help me to do something to let people know SCA is real, the pain hurts, and they ought to be doing something about it here in Baltimore.'" The black doctors were no better than the white, according to Clayburn, in terms of helping the public to understand this disease; "it had been overlooked." Today, Clayburn is a national board member of the SCA; it was because of her efforts that the association in the Baltimore area, funded by HEW, formed and now has offices in five Baltimore-area hospitals. Research, public activities, plans are checked with Clayburn's association. "The City of Baltimore literally does nothing to do with SCA without contacting me first," she says.

Sickle-cell volunteer activities gave her publicity at the same time that her success on the airwaves was growing. Mary Clayburn was paid to be a radio broadcaster. But she also decided to work for nothing to gain more intensive knowledge of the media field. "The possibilities and the equipment where I was working were limited. I wanted to get into news functions, and I had to go somewhere else to learn how. How to write it, read it, how to gather the news together. So I picked the largest station in the city." She offered to work in the news area. "The engineers were very happy to allow me to go into WCBM, the Metromedia station here, and work with the men in the newsroom." It was a twenty-four-hour operation, so she could go in after her two part-time jobs, for she still worked at the library during the hours her husband was home with the children. "The people at WCBM showed me how to write, how to coordinate, how you take news off the wire service, how you call in a hot story, how to pick up news coming from other states, and how to feed news to other states. For about five months I worked on different shifts, night and day, and I wasn't paid. They were very nice to me.

"Then I wanted to get some experience in television." She went to channel 2, the CBS affiliate. "I did the same thing there, and eventually worked as a producer of a musical variety show. They called me the talent coordinator. Find talent, tell them what to wear, when to show up, what to do, what to say, then I gave the script to the moderator." Once a week for a year, with no pay. "I never really thought about being paid. I used to love to watch my name roll by in the credits. I got expensive training." She got a career. "Right." Perhaps her television colleagues saw in her what the WWIN program director, Don Brooks, does: "Mary is different from the majority of women—she is career-oriented and she handles her job in that way. She doesn't ask for special favors from the guys."

Instead, she worked in payment for training as her career

began to blossom. She hardly remembers all she got involved with. Commercials, TV projects, the sickle-cell cause. There were, unfortunately, new happenings in her marriage as well.

"I don't know when it started. Mack appeared proud of me at first. He would tell people to listen to the program, listen to the interviews, and when I came over to this new job [at WWIN] he was still very, very proud of me. But then we started to go to meetings, to functions, directly related to this job—one-hundred-dollar-a-plate dinners, Agnew was going to be there, Lucy Johnson, Humphrey—he started to try to upstage me. My sister mentioned it first; I thought she was picking on him. . . .

"He didn't know when to stop talking and start listening. He asked questions that didn't make sense. He embarrassed me. Our friends were fewer and fewer. . . .

"It was my SCA involvement that won for me the Advertising Woman Award—locally—and the Advertising Woman of the Year, nationally, a year later," and Clayburn remembers the night she was presented with the local award. Her husband was sitting on the dais, "and friends and relatives noted that they couldn't tell if he was happy or miserable. He hadn't attained his goals and here I was, on my way. . . . We went downhill from there. I'd do a show, I'd be on television, and he'd be home. 'How did you like it?' I'd ask him, and he would say, 'Oh, I was busy with the children.' Did he become involved with another woman? That was rumored. But I was never sure."

Then one day her husband announced: "I quit. I want to find myself. I want to do something. I've had it. I've worked my last day." Clayburn shakes her head: "From that day, it went down —fast. I didn't want to go home after work, I developed headaches. It was terrible. He was home, day and night. Finding himself. He got into a depression, I got into a depression. His was probably because of my success. Mine was because of his giving up.

"My father was dead and my sisters were on my side but just weren't helping me make the decisions." She traveled to North Carolina to visit with supportive friends, who said, " 'We will help

The Clayburns, the night Mary was presented the award for Advertising Woman of the Year.

you as much as we can—we'll back you up'; that was all I needed."

She stopped in Washington, D.C., on her way back to Baltimore, "and I told my uncle I was going to leave my husband. He reminded me, 'You're the first one in the family to ever divorce. Our family does not believe in divorce.' He made me feel real bad." Mary recalls her father's original resistance to her marriage, which lasted thirteen years, until 1972. "He was right. But we stayed together as long as my father was alive." She still expresses her guilt over the breakup: "Did I try to help Mack? Did I try as hard as I could? As long as I can feel it's not my fault . . ."

Her husband wouldn't leave their house: "He said *he* wasn't the one with the problem. We weren't talking about love then. We played a game of the first person to the bed, got the bed. The

other one slept on the living room couch. I remember going to
bed at six so I'd have the bed. Isn't that crazy?"

Her children were seven and eleven as she moved into an
apartment around the corner, "so the children could walk back
home and see Mack and still have the same friends." She left
everything in the house, didn't have pots and pans to cook with,
no furniture. "Some girlfriends of mine came to the rescue,
bringing me all sorts of things." Her husband remarried soon
after, "a much younger woman. Men after a breakup seem to
have new energy, don't you think?"

She was energetic herself. Shortly before her separation she
was hired for a new position, public affairs director for Baltimore's WWIN. "I can do this job if I'm given a shot," she had
said and then proved it. Her Sunday gospel show includes reading church announcements and coordinating activities and
music. On Saturday nights, she interviews congressmen, mayors,
Muhammad Ali, Billy Dee Williams, Isaac Hayes. And according
to the station manager, Shelton Earp, she does her homework:
"Oh yes indeed, she does. She does not grope or hesitate in her
ad lib work. . . . She can be very vivacious and she can be mild.
. . . She's very pleasant. Mary gets along with people. Logic,
common sense—all those qualities that are necessary for her
particular position. It's not an easy job. She's just done an incredible job for us and we're deeply proud of her. I feel she has
contributed mightily to this organization in every way. . . .

"Her job requires her to talk with myriad organizations in the
community—literally hundreds of individuals—and she is so involved that she has to be diplomatic to stay in this job. There's
a plethora of announcements that we get swamped with [there
are about 200 black churches alone in Baltimore], a station with
an audience as large as ours. And we can't run everything for
everybody, so she has to be selective, and that in itself makes her
diplomatic. Being a public affairs person in the black community
is different from anything else you've ever seen in your life. The
black community is demanding, there are often two or three

aspects to everything we deal with—a pro and a con to every-thing. You've got to be a diplomat, but you also have to stand on the side you think to be right."

Always supporting that which is right, Clayburn, interviewer, gospel disk jockey, public affairs director, also free-lances for radio and TV. For example, she ran a talent show, "Jubilee," on Baltimore's NBC channel 11. She does an interview show on ABC's channel 13 and judged an epilepsy telethon. She modeled for a Good Will fashion show, and was the force behind a half-hour TV movie on handicaps for the City of Baltimore.

The high school graduate clerking at the library has come a long way. Earp says, "She just simply does her work, and I don't know how she does it. She doesn't let her illness handicap her in life." She still has severe SCA crises about twice a year, when she must be hospitalized. "Other than that, I handle it myself," says Clayburn, although frequently the pain will cause her to be in bed for several days. But not only did she not let her disease stop her, she turned it into a career stepping stone.

Consistently this divorced black woman, suffering from a life-long disease while raising two sons, sees problems as advantages. The naïve teenager, unqualified for anything above clerical work, turned her library experience—"all those people I met"—into an excellent background for TV and radio work. For now she has everything to do with the public, including access to the ear of the white community. "Anybody coming into town to do any-thing that they want a black audience to know about must contact me. I really don't have hangups about why I'm here—to serve the best interests of the community. It's not my voice; it belongs to the people." Thus her ethnic heritage becomes a positive factor as she works for the black community, is a role model for young people. When Mary learned that high school student Michelle Singletary was interested in a radio career, she called the young-ster's principal and arranged for Michelle to become her assist-ant. Michelle appreciates the older woman's attention: "She's an idol, but I can still look at her as a person. She's honest. You really don't find that too often. She's always willing to help you if you're willing to help yourself. I'm just glad to be working for her. It's unbelievable!"

Clayburn, at first inexperienced in the media, volunteered her free time so she could learn. And, when she needed a third-class engineer's license to continue as a disk jockey, "I went right back to those same people [who had taught her about the news and TV business] and said, 'I don't understand the dials.' They gave me a crash course." Does Mary Clayburn have an aptitude for electronics? Did she know anything beforehand? She shakes her head, "No," and adds, "I still don't. When a plug comes out I call someone." WWIN Program Director Brooks says, "Mary's not mechanically inclined or technically minded. If you tell her to set a lever to five and it's moved to seven, she's not sure if she should turn it back to five." And he laughs. Her feeling: "To know your limit is what's necessary." And to know how to turn liabilities into assets.

An award winner many times over—two City of Baltimore Citizen's Citations, a historical society award, first black woman to win an award from the Advertising Federation, leader in Leonia against SCA, Delta Sigma Theta award in the area of community development, on a distinctive honor role of outstanding women, Certificate of Appreciation from the United Methodist Church, Community Health Council of Maryland certificate, National Association of Negro Business and Professional Women's Clubs award, Citizens Committee for Voter Education award, Concentrated Employment Program Community Service award, and honored by a Mary Clayburn Day in Baltimore—proclaimed by Mayor William Donald Schaeffer.

Yet when Clayburn talks about life's achievements, she mentions her children first. Mark, after graduating from a prestigious Baltimore high school, attends the Ohio Institute of Technology. Son Myron is in high school. General manager Earp says, "Mary's raised two fine boys," and an old friend says Mary talks about her "baby son" constantly. Susie Wood adds, "When you're raising

Mary Clayburn on the air, shortly after her election as vice-president of the Northern region of the National Association for Television and Radio Artists. News American Photo by John Davis

two boys alone and you keep them out of jail and a roof over their heads and their stomachs filled, you've done a good job." Clayburn seems to have made fine work of everything she's touched.

Within the parameters her parents instilled, she enjoys a fulfilling life. Her friends, professional associates, and business superiors comment on the outgoing, feminine, moralistic woman:

> She gets upset if somebody else is recognized for something that she did. Which is normal. She can get highly upset. She's not looking for recognition but at the same time, she's looking for fairness, if it comes about.

> Mary doesn't boast. It's a good way to be. There are people like that. It's like the person who gives $50,000 to the Cancer Society but says, "Don't mention my name."

> She's deep. She is doing a lot, she's on many boards, but unless you pry, you don't know it. And then, Mary is the kind of person who may be sharing it with someone special.

There is someone in Mary's life: "I'm dating a guy I went to elementary school with. I don't really want to get married. Not now." She and her friend "are compatible; our upbringing is very similar. His father was the strength of his family too."

Mary Clayburn looks toward her future and asserts, "I always like a challenge. . . . Why, when the opportunity presented itself, I took it, then I tried to improve myself. I could have sat back on what I had, and not tried to learn more about broadcasting, the other facets of it. But I wanted to know. Even though I never thought I'd do news, I wanted to know about it because it's all related. . . . Learn as much as you can about whatever it is you're interested in. Inspiration doesn't come to those who wait for it, 'when this is done,' 'when the time is right.' Get to it *now*. Work on it. Today. Start now."

How Mary Clayburn Did It

1. Suffering from a debilitating disease, Clayburn decided to not let her sickle-cell anemia control her. "She doesn't let her illness handicap her in life," says Shelton Earp.

2. Working for the library system "put me in touch with so many different kinds of people." Facing racism, she chose to understand it, work to change individual prejudices, and gain knowledge herself.

3. As her children were born, she continued to work part time, when her husband was home and, later, while her youngest was with a sitter for short periods.

4. Realizing she could not significantly advance at the library and wanting change, she walked into a neighborhood radio station and asked for work, although a job had not been advertised.

5. When the opportunity came—she could be a part-time gospel disk jockey—she rose to the challenge, teaching herself the necessary mechanical aspects of communications at her kitchen table.

6. "My voice was always a negative. I just turned it around." A black woman with a deep vocal range became a disk jockey at a black-oriented station. Negatives into positives.

7. She created jobs within her job. As an SCA advocate, she became visible. As an SCA victim, she used her personal knowledge of the disease as a stepping stone.

8. She searched for the opportunity to work without pay in TV and news broadcasting. "They allowed me to work. I got expensive training. . . . Learn as much as you can about whatever you're interested in," says Clayburn. Even if it means months of hard work with no salary.

9. As her career switch gained momentum, the newly divorced woman continued to raise Mark and Myron, with love and attention.

10. Aiming for a more prestigious position, she insisted, "I can do this job if I'm given a shot," then she proved it. Self-assurance, assertiveness, and, finally, delivering on the promises.

11. She shares her position's prestige with others on their way up. A job for a black teenager, a word to a friend about an opening: Concern for others eventually has a positive impact on Clayburn.

8

Ladylike and Liberated

Marilyn Miller Stiefvater is the broker-owner of a thirteen-person realty firm in the small New York village of Pelham. She's also the wife of a man she divorced. She once married Richard Stiefvater, they split up, and Mrs. Stiefvater lived alone for three years while Dick was married to another woman. After he and his second wife separated, Dick and Marilyn remarried each other.

Marilyn Stiefvater's deep velvetlike voice, reminiscent of Lauren Bacall's smoky tones, rises as she explains that her marital experiences are relevant to her success in real estate. For while a grass widow, she formed and began to build her business to its present impressive proportions. But her early adult years were spent as a mother, and as Mrs. Richard Stiefvater.

When Marilyn first began dating Dick, he was working in their upstate New York hometown of Utica for Marilyn's grandfather's corporation. Dick was at first unaware he was courting the boss's granddaughter; when they decided to wed, he quit. He would not be accused of marrying Marilyn to elevate himself professionally.

Marilyn's well-to-do family was prominent in the town, and, when she was a child, "anything we wanted was provided," within reason. The tall, large-boned woman with a big smile and white sparkling teeth remembers that "Dad was a first-rate insurance man," but intelligent, unaggressive Mr. Miller lacked a sense of humor. Very stern. Characteristically clicking her fingers for emphasis, she admits, "I'm a bit that way . . . quite a lot that way." It was her mother she was close to. "I couldn't get along with my father. We always argued. He was always right. I was always right. There was a stalemate. He was a terribly difficult man." All spoken in that polished soft voice while exuding, according to a friend, "warmth, sweetness, femininity." Marilyn continues: "It was that whole syndrome: Mother did whatever Dad wanted. His wish was her command. Always, always, always."

There were four births in the family within five years; Marilyn, born in 1931, has a younger brother and twin sisters. "Without trying terribly hard," Marilyn excelled in school. She was probably too popular with the boys, she says, and smiles at the memory. But "I remember resenting so much the lack of praise from my father." When she was accepted into the National Honor Society, "never once did he say, 'I'm proud of you.' Never ever." His admiration was for her face and statuesque five-foot nine-inch figure rather than her achievements. Perhaps

Cheerleading champs of Oneida County, New York. Captain Marilyn Miller is in the center.

that's why she did not think beyond nurse's training, she feels today.

After graduation from high school, Marilyn entered a local college, then transferred to Columbia University to become a nurse. The forthright woman with short reddish brown hair has an assured air as she tilts her head and remembers male patients nicknaming her "Dimples." Her supervisor was scandalized. Not dignified. Nurse Miller should be referred to as "Miss Miller."

Richard Stiefvater began dating Miss Miller while she was in nurse's training. When asked if there were other serious relationships before she met Dick, Marilyn answers, "That's a sore subject. I can still cry when I think about it." In school in New York City, Marilyn was dating a University of Rochester medical student. They went together for years, flying to see each other. "He was the most fantastic person I've ever met. *Madly* in love." Jim Brown and Marilyn dated in 1954 and '55 until he went into the service. She expected to marry him before he departed. His feeling was that the army experience was no life for a wife. Her heart broken as he left—she says he essentially ended the relationship—she began to date Dick.

Two days prior to Dick and Marilyn's wedding, a twelve-page letter from Brown arrived, explaining, according to her, the "whys and wherefores." He had made a terrible mistake. He wanted to see her. Dick insisted she do so, but the proud bride-to-be decided not to and never answered Brown's letter. (Brown, now married, practices medicine in upstate New York.)

The Stiefvater's oldest child, a boy, was born nine months later. Marilyn, working in a Utica hospital, resigned to care for her child. Their son was followed by two more children: "I stayed home with them, and home with them, and *home with them.*"

As the children arrived, Dick began working for an oil company. Extra hours spent with the corporation were, in Marilyn's view, simply time away from the family. She resented his heavy traveling schedule and overtime. As he was elevated from a Getty Oil salesman to advertising manager and sales promotion director, his resultant job transfers caused the Steifvaters to relocate continually. "That corporate climb up the ladder just takes its toll on *so* many families, and I'm sure it did on ours," says Marilyn.

As her youngest child began kindergarten, she decided to work in the mornings. But "Dick didn't want me working and spending *any* time away from home." His attitude was that a woman's place was in the home, yet she could no longer spend "*all* that time in the home. Morning, noon, and night." Again, Marilyn was faced with a man who, like her father, refused to acknowledge her intellectual needs and capabilities. A friend feels "Marilyn is not geared to stay home—she'd go crazy. She hates to clean; she doesn't like to cook." And not a social person or a club joiner,

Marilyn Stiefvater as a young mother, in 1965.

Marilyn chose—against Dick's wishes—to utilize her nursing degree working four mornings a week for a local pediatrician. Dick was waiting, and almost hoping, for trouble, according to Marilyn. The first time Marilyn arrived home moments late and their child had to wait on the doorstep, her husband became enraged. She stopped working for the pediatrician at the end of the year. But the resentment grew.

They were then renting a home in Pelham, New York, having recently moved from California, the thirteenth relocation in as many years. Marilyn finally said to her husband: " 'No more. The children need security. If Getty transfers you again, I'm not going.' I finally just kind of blew my stack." The moves, in combination with his refusal to discuss his business day with her, slowly destroyed the marriage. Marilyn felt, "If I had to stay home all day, the *least* he owed me was to share his life with me." The marriage ended in 1968; the divorcee was thirty-seven, with children twelve, ten, and seven.

Marilyn, with $425 a month child-support payments, began employment hunting and got a job in a local gift shop "while I thought things out." She did not wish to continue in medicine.

One day over lunch, while she was still employed at the retail store, a realtor-acquaintance mentioned an opening in her office, said that she and her boss had discussed Marilyn's attributes, and wondered if she'd like the position: "It's funny," says Marilyn. "It was something that *always* kind of appealed to me and I had actually discussed it with Dick, and said, 'I'd like to go into real estate.' And his comment was, 'Well, that would mean you'd have to work weekends.' In other words, 'forget it.' And I thought, it probably would mean weekends, and the children are small and I just can't do it. So as soon as he left [when the Stiefvaters were divorced], it was interesting that . . ." she accepted the offer, contingent upon a two-week trial period.

She loved it. "The office was a happy place." Her boss's daughter, Josie Magnani, remembers her father raving about the new saleswoman: "He thought she was the brightest gal going. And he didn't think much of most people." Stiefvater recalls, "It was almost understood from the time I went with him" that she would eventually buy the business. "He said, when he interviewed me the first time, that he was interested in retiring and was looking for someone who was capable of taking the office over. Now he may very well have said that to everybody else in the office. But he did say it to me. So that was something that was in the back of my mind for quite some time." If he had not retired when he did, "I'd have gone and opened my own office. I knew I could do it."

Marilyn reflects: "It was all kind of lucky really." Luck? A friend cuts through, "Come on Marilyn, they came and asked you." Her talents were noticeable, and Josie Magnani—her father sold his business to Marilyn, and Josie now works for Stiefvater—states, "Most gals in real estate don't want all that responsibility. You have to be very pro-business. Most gals don't have the time to dedicate to it."

Marilyn had the motivation and, now divorced, the freedom. From 1968 until 1971, her business began to develop financially as she personally blossomed. "Those years after we divorced were especially fruitful for me. Mentally, physically. I felt younger. I was much more alive." Did she feel more attractive? "Oh, much prettier, much prettier."

A friend, Rusty Lotti, says Stiefvater is "too honest, too trusting." These qualities were combined with a sharp, logical mind and the desire to excel, remnants of a teenage need to convince her father, and later her husband, that she had a brain. Marilyn, with all the ingredients for success intact, was on her way.

R. Andrew Stiefvater, Marilyn's eldest child at twenty-four, twists his face into a lopsided expression as is his father's habit, and thinks carefully about his mother: "I admire her a lot for what she did. Real estate was a new field to her; she went into it cold and did well from the start. And it didn't take her long to do *very* well at it. I think that's pretty neat. It's unusual—I think it's more than unusual—for a woman of my mother's generation."

Question: If a man of your mother's generation had done it, would you be as impressed?

Answer: I would still think it was special. I don't think a man would have been home for years, then have to go out to support the children, and been forced to do it as well as my mother did. If it had happened that way to a man, I think it would have been just as unusual.

Andy Stiefvater is not the only one impressed with Marilyn Stiefvater. Her friend, Mrs. Lotti, speaks of Marilyn's open friendliness in business and in personal relationships: "It's always there. She's totally unthreatening. Everyone feels comfortable around her. I know she wouldn't hustle anyone." And a business associate states, "She's very personable plus has brightness to back it up. She's got it all."

She certainly seemed to know what she was doing when, the day she took over the business, she placed an unusual ad:

CATASTROPHIC COLONIAL!!

A dreadful house of sinister aspect that time and decay have not softened. 8 rooms with large kitchen and bath (hot and cold running water). Wallpaper hangs rather dankly. Otherwise, not too much wrong with it. For those with time, energy and some money . . .

Stiefvater laughs. "It sold the house that day," and continues: "My business became as much my life as my former life used to be. I enjoyed every single minute of it. It was fascinating to me. I was so totally absorbed. The children were old enough" for her to be immersed, without guilt, in her chosen career. She had a social life as well; from 1968 until 1971, realtor Stiefvater dated, yet decided not to continue the couple of potentially serious relationships.

Her ex-husband, Richard, in the meantime married a twenty-six-year-old woman about two years after he and Marilyn, now thirty-eight, divorced. Yet one day he asked Marilyn to discuss the children at his apartment. When she arrived, Dick explained that his short-lived marriage was over and, Marilyn says, "We had one of the nicest evenings we ever had." They spent a month together on Fire Island with their children during that summer of 1971: "I saw a lot of changes in him." A significant difference was Dick's acceptance of Marilyn's need to have a career and recognition of her business ability. Later that year, they remarried, three years after being divorced.

Six months after their second marriage, Dick left Getty; his ambition had evaporated. With Dick out of work, Marilyn became the sole breadwinner. "I thought it was going to be temporary. It did not turn out that way." Her expressive face is troubled. "The tables were kind of turned." She twists one of her many jade rings.

Womanly Marilyn, a chain smoker who feels that aggressive unfeminine women constantly hold a lighted cigarette—"It seems to go hand in hand"—and dislikes the fact that she is a smoker, lights another as she talks about Dick, an excellent cook who spent his days collecting recipes from female friends. He became a gourmet chef. "He dug a little hole for himself," according to his wife, who did not like to entertain: "I didn't have the time or energy. Even with my 'wife' doing the work." Yet she often came home tired from a day's work to discover there would be guests in an hour. This used to be *his* position coming home from the office.

An acquaintance feels "Marilyn dwarfed Dick. She had to carry the family's financial load for too long."

Forty-nine-year-old Marilyn believes it doesn't work for the man and wife of her generation to switch roles. If they were both in their twenties . . . "But we are still living in the 1950s in many respects. . . . Terribly degrading," she says of her husband's situation.

Marilyn muses, "We had a lovely rosy [second marriage] life going for the first three, four years, but going into the fifth, then sixth, seventh, I could see us reverting to old patterns." At the same time that their marriage is once again disintegrating, her Pelham real estate business is flourishing.

Marilyn M. Stiefvater Real Estate is located in the closest West- chester County bedroom area to New York City. A group of wealthy communities with a varied ethnic makeup, the Pelhams are home to the president of Bloomingdale's, Patrick Moynihan, the head of Alitalia Airlines, Finland's and the British West In- dies' UN representatives, for example.

Stiefvater's office sells millions of dollars of homes, land, and buildings each year in the Pelhams. Her gross business income is in excess of $200,000. As the boss, she is trying to become less involved with direct sales, although she personally sold eight houses during the past year. Stiefvater's company is the top real estate business of the seven in the Pelhams, where she serves as

The Stiefvater sales force. Marilyn, standing, third from right.

the Westchester County Realty Board's president.

This patient woman, whose incongruous nickname in college was Flash, travels from her home to work in minutes. Her office, complete with awning and lots of plants, overlooks Pelham's park and Town Hall. She begins work at her desk, where a plant, several appraisal sheets, contract forms, and a picture of her three children are placed. With the Town of Pelham map on the wall behind her, Stiefvater works at an easygoing, constant rate in an organized fashion. She usually eats a sandwich at her desk and might be interrupted as a woman employee comes in with a serious problem. The boss, in her low direct voice: "*I* will handle it."

"Attractive? Oh yes!" says an employee. "All the men—are you kidding?—just adore her, rave about her." One tries to pin down Marilyn's appeal: ". . . the way she carries herself, presents herself —very assuredly . . ." Another male friend feels it's her personality rather than her good looks.

And her attitude. One of her children says Marilyn is flexible, makes the best of any situation, and he speaks of her "personal" voice and her more assertive deeper "business" tones. Son Andy says his mother is intelligent. "I think extremely." And intellectual? "Yeah." Feminine? "I think so. I think so." Assertive? "Yes." Aggressive? "Yes." But feminine? "Honestly! Honestly! I don't want to make her out like superwoman, but she is feminine and aggressive and she is assertive. I think those things can make *anybody* do pretty well at whatever they want."

Marilyn seems to concur. She says that many of her female employees unrealistically expect to find the real estate business, traditionally a female occupation, a part-time job, not something that will separate them from their family. But, says Stiefvater, "after about a year the *changes I see.* I've seen the maturity come about in these women who are so used to staying home, being told what to do by their husbands. They're beginning to tell their husbands to go jump in the creek. Self-assurance comes with age, and it's amazing to see those changes. I expect that, in the long run, the marriages will probably be healthier marriages." She smoothes what she refers to as her liberated woman's hairstyle. Minimal upkeep.

A female employee comments on the Stiefvater professional touch: "Men don't sell a home as well as a woman. Women customers are interested in 'Can Johnny get to school from here?' and 'Can I cook in this kitchen?' and women have a more personal approach with these customers." Marilyn in particular. "Oh, she's marvelous! Really. She is! Extremely patient but also businesslike. She's got the right amount of everything. Personable, conscientious. Yes, everything." Everything. Except a happy home life.

"When I was very young, every time I broke a wishbone," says son Andy, "I wished my parents [then divorced] would get back together. I think I kind of always expected it." And now that they are again heading toward separation? "Now? I don't think I ex-

Stiefvater in action in 1979, in her office, flanked by Deputy Mayor and Village Trustee John Caulway; Kay Woodward, Pelham attorney (in plaid suit); and Jean Hardy, licensed Stiefvater broker. Photo by Mary Jane Worobel

pected it. I'm not glad for it, obviously. I don't feel very good
about it, I wish it wasn't happening."

An old friend, Mario Lotti, described Marilyn as conservative,
righteous, a divider of right from wrong. And as her son speaks
in her presence, Marilyn is distressed; her troubles, another divorce are unsettling. But then he adds, "She makes the best of
any situation. And she enjoys being by herself . . . doing what she
wants to do. I think she could live very well by herself. I picture
her having a very good time. I don't mean to say that I don't think
she'll also suffer by living alone. . . ."

Stiefvater, a winner in her own eyes, has made that final decision but has trouble implementing it. Rusty Lotti on her friend:
"Marilyn amazes me. She is such a well-put-together person in
every way. And she is so decisive. But with Dick . . ."

Marilyn says she tends to wait for things to happen within her
personal life. She talks of ending her "perpetual holding pattern"
and probably selling the home where her children were raised,
perhaps when she and Dick finally separate. Her son Andy and
Dick continue, for the moment, to live in her eclectic 1870 house,
stuffed with curios and antique Miller family furniture. After a
day's work, she walks in through a delightful Victorian country
kitchen with white "public" bathroom ceramic tile, red and white
plaid wallpaper, antique dentist's bureau, and pressed-tin ceiling
and states, emphatically, perhaps bitterly: "If I had my way, I'd
design a house that didn't have a kitchen. I like to eat but I don't
like to prepare food or do anything with it." As she speaks, her
son, preparing his dinner, opens a defunct dishwasher, now a
breadbox. His mother throws away nothing. She laughs at herself.

Marilyn describes herself as "happy and fulfilled" in spite of
her problems. And she believes that if she is serene, her family
ultimately will be, but "I hate to think that the second time
around will go down the drain too."

Yet she says, "I really don't believe in fate." She takes responsibility for her present position, professionally and personally.

"Luck and circumstances combined and probably a strong will of my own (which I like to hide)" led this now-independent gentle-woman to answer, when questioned as to whether she needs a man, "No, I don't think I really do."

How Marilyn Stiefvater Did It

1. Marilyn recognized that as her youngest entered school, she needed involvement outside the home, although her husband could not accept this.

2. Her marriage ended when she was thirty-seven. Marilyn considered her options and saw that her choice of a nursing vocation was a mistake.

3. When a realty position was offered to her on a trial basis, she accepted, considering it a full-time profession, now possible as her children reached their teen years.

4. Her boss explained that he wished to retire. Marilyn chose to assume that he meant to sell his business to her and, with dedication, worked toward that goal.

5. Her desire to own her own real estate business was strong; if this particular one were not eventually available to her, she would open a new one—she had an alternative plan.

6. "I knew I could do it." She believed in herself.

7. As she was successful in the marketplace, her self-esteem grew. "I felt younger. I was much more alive."

8. She was patient, businesslike, in empathy with her female customers. Marilyn used all her particular womanly abilities to the fullest—rather than trying to emulate men in business. She placed unique ads, was conscientious. And she made money.

9

Oh Happy Day!

The instructor stands at the head of the class of leotard-clad women: "And as you turn, keep your knees bent with your weight on your left foot, and extend your right hip out as far as you can." The belly dance teacher then demonstrates as the class watches.

In the third row, fourth from the left, stands fifty-three-year-old Alison Cheek, a full-figured, gray-haired woman. This smiling matron, a parent to four children, became a father as well as a mother when, at forty-seven, she was ordained as the first woman Episcopal priest.

After her first sermon as a priest, a man came out of the church, shook the Reverend Cheek's hand, and asked, "Shall I call you Mother?" Alison says in her soft Australian accent: "He was being smart-assed. And I said—softly—'If you have need of one, certainly.'" Constantly asked this sort of question, Alison says, "I seem to have developed a *spiel*. A little record goes on and I say, 'As far as I'm concerned, there are only brothers and sisters in the Church, and I've always felt it was quite appropriate for Christians to call each other by their Christian names. But if you're only comfortable with a title, by all means, call me Father.'" She giggles.

What motivated this woman—with her short, naturally wavy hair, casually cut, and an outgoing, no-nonsense manner—to begin a second life after years as a wife and mother? And what

Unitarian Church. He died when I was in my early teens, and he has never ceased to be present to me."

The influences of her parents and grandparents were complemented by a childless couple—Auntie Doll and Uncle Bert—who had bought a parcel of Alison's parents' land. "From Bert I absorbed a sense of self-worth. He broke through role stereotypes. Gentle and courtly though he was, he had a strong sentiment about the equality of the sexes and believed that girls should be given every opportunity offered to boys. He encouraged me to be who I am."

Alison's sturdy hands, with neatly clipped nails, move as she speaks, accentuating her words. Because she was a bright child and learned to read quickly, "my mother . . . had the ambition that I should go to the University, which was unusual for a girl." Only about one out of ten went to college from her fruit-growing district, and the number of girls was minuscule.

She was the first in her family to go to college. (Her brother died in World War II when Alison was seventeen.) "It was my mother's gift to me that she made me believe that I could get my BA. I'm indebted to her for my tertiary education."

At the University of Adelaide, majoring in economics and political science, Alison Mary Western met Bruce Cheek, her economics tutor. After her graduation in 1947, she quips, she "opted for domesticity." She left the Australian land that she loved, she comments in mock italics, for "that man! That man!" Immediately after the war the newly married couple traveled to the United States, where Bruce Cheek became the first Peter Brooks Saltonstall scholar at Harvard, a fellowship awarded to individuals from the Pacific islands.

During the years the couple lived in the Cambridge area, their first child, named for his father, was born, "twelve thousand miles away from home, my mother, and good advice," Alison recalls. She stayed home and took care of the baby. They were sorely in need of funds. But as an alien, she could not work. Although strapped, they enjoyed several pleasant years while Bruce attended Harvard and their second child, Jonathan, was born.

When Bruce Cheek was offered a position in Australia, he decided to accept. Back home, their third child, Timothy, was born, and Alison converted to the Episcopalian religion. "And I became an avid reader of Gesell and Ilg."

In 1957 Bruce was hired by a Washington, D.C., organization, and once again the Cheeks packed up and moved to the United States. Bruce never returned to academic economics; he stayed at Washington's World Bank for twenty years at a job involving worldwide travel. His wife often joined him; she recalls a particularly exciting trip to Africa. During these years, the early sixties, Alison, with three young children, became a PTA officer and the Christian education chairman at her local parish church in Annendale, Virginia, on the outskirts of the District of Columbia.

Mrs. Bruce Cheek on her Virginia lawn, with her youngest. Pre-bloom.

And while they were living in Virginia their daughter, Bronwen, was born. Alison was then thirty-one.

It was during her years in Virginia that she became deeply involved with her religion. Although she had been intrigued with the subject in college—she recalls grappling with Schweitzer's theological philosophy—her interest resurfaced when she saw a Virginia Theological Seminary movie explaining the educational experience men had there. "I watched that film and I felt that there was where I belonged. It was kind of an unnerving thing." She recalls going home, Bruce opening the door, looking at her face, and saying, "Yes? What happened?" In a dazed voice she said, "Oh. I watched that film on the seminary." He thought a moment and responded, "Yes, I think you should go." She hadn't gotten that far. "I hadn't put any reason to it. It was a very intuitive thing. I went step by step, by painful step."

Prior to her decision to attempt to enter a seminary, "The only jobs I had had were part-time secretarial work and tutoring in economics at Adelaide." And as a wife and mother to four children.

It was one thing to decide to become educated at the seminary and another actually to enter this male bailiwick. With her parish priest's help, she was presented to the admissions committee, to be educated within her religion with no conscious desire to become a priest. It was coincidental that the committee had just accepted one woman for the first time and thought it would be sensible for her to have a companion.

In an article she wrote years later, she spoke of her reaction: "It admitted me—a woman! It allowed me to extend my course over six years instead of three so I could raise four young children at the same time. It has taken me forever to stop feeling grateful and to start feeling outraged that I felt so grateful. Never again can I allow myself to be defined by the church as an inferior being whose sexuality needs to be voted upon.

"I came to seminary when I was thirty-six. That first year I would drop Bronwen off at kindergarten, then whiz down to

Alexandria, do two courses, leap into the car to pick her up." The next year Bronwen stayed for lunch and, "I could fit in three courses. Once I tried to take four but found I could not carry four with four children."

She recalls her fellow students sarcastically asking, " 'You one of these women who wants to be a *priestess?*' So I really have to thank my brothers for putting the idea of becoming a priest in my mind. . . . I thought I was doing something that would be a preparation for the time when I didn't really have to be at home. . . .

"Certainly I was just as competent as anybody else at that seminary. If not more so." Her success at her graduate education thrilled Bruce outwardly; during these years he typed her term papers and helped with the house and the children. Yet, as he headed toward what she terms his mid-life crisis, their marriage began to feel the effects of his age, her career, or perhaps both. "That's when things began to change. For that's when I really began to grow." Bruce suffered a heart attack the spring she graduated, and slowly recovered.

Her new career was to affect more than her immediate family. With Alison's graduation—she was awarded the master of divinity in 1969—began the sequence of events that would bring this woman worldwide renown in her struggle to be ordained as a priest.

Her first position after graduation was at the historic Christ Church in Alexandria as a parish staff member. While still at the seminary, she had taken a course at the Washington Institute for Pastoral Psychotherapy and, while working at the Christ Church, was asked to be on the staff of an adjunct of the Washington Institute, the Pastoral Counseling and Consultation Centers. She left Christ Church and worked at the Counseling and Consultation Centers for three years.

In January of 1972, while working at the Centers as a pastoral counselor, Alison was ordained as a deacon and was employed sporadically at her local parish church in Virginia, St. Alban's.

She feels her decision to become a priest crystallized at this time. Angry that she could be a deacon and not a priest, she resented serving the Episcopalian Church—for she felt it treated women as second-class citizens. She felt "a tremendous urge to be autonomous, to stand on my own two feet, to have space." She resigned from the Pastoral Counseling and Consultation Centers and opened a private practice as a pastoral psychotherapist.

As her resentment grew and her career goals became clearer to her, her marriage suffered. Her husband continued to encourage her, was "*tremendously* supportive and *enormously* helpful, still it was a hard adjustment for him." As she found her calling, he was considering his options and recognizing he had few. The problem had little to do with his being married to a woman who was finding her own place in the world, Alison feels, but it was rather a reaction to his own aging and the possibility of death.

Her psychotherapy career required her to go through analysis. Bruce, during the aftermath of his heart attack, sought counseling as well. Eventually they got into a couples' group, and in the process, says Alison, "We both changed a lot."

She wrote at that time: "In claiming my inheritance, defining myself, trusting myself, and exploring ideas and sharing myself vulnerably in public situations, I have perhaps grown more in the past two years than at any other time in my adult years."

It was then 1974, the year that Alison Cheek became a public person.

In the Episcopal church a person must first be a deacon—an apprentice for the priesthood—for six months before priestly ordination. But many deacons never become priests, although a deacon is essentially a working priest on a lower salary. Although there is no Episcopalian canon law forbidding the ordination of women deacons to the priesthood, women had unsuccessfully tried to become priests for decades.

When the Church refused to ordain Alison, she considered leaving Episcopalianism, perhaps to join another denomination: "I decided I didn't want to be the official representative of a church that was treating women this way. Then out of the blue came a call from one of my sister deacons saying some retired bishops were going to ordain a few women in Philadelphia and would I like to be included? All I could say for about five minutes was, 'Wow.' " She accepted immediately.

"I still live in the repercussions of that event.

"I was the first woman publicly to function as a priest in an Episcopalian church. At the time I wasn't even aware I was making history. Never expected public interest. Was outwardly apolitical. It was *such* a frightening thing for me. I got thrust into all this publicity. It was *so* unexpected." She became essentially an outlaw within her religion, participating in two public ecclesiastical trials, publicity, and speaking engagements, at which she steadfastly took a stand on a moral issue—"the recognition of the full humanity of women.

"I was surprised to be named one of *Time* magazine's 'Women of the Year' but even more surprised, having been named, to discover that I felt at home with that, and that I valued for myself the struggle of the spirit." *Time* called her "the defiant deacon" and stated "boat rocking did not come easily to the Rev. Alison Cheek," who was quoted at the time—1976—as saying, "I am convinced that the only crime I have committed in this matter is to have been born female."

During the period when there was such a brouhaha going on in connection with her ordination, she looked forward to babysitting for her two grandchildren one night a week. She sighs. "It was so *normal.*"

The actual ordination completed an emotionally packed day. The service was televised. "A woman who makes vestments made me a chasuble—a eucharistic vestment, a cloak worn by the celebrant of the eucharist for mass," with a patchwork print appliquéd on the yellow back, stating "Oh Happy Day" surrounded with oversized butterflies.

The ordination was soon followed by religious trials of the clergy who had ordained her, and, she says, "It was like Watergate."

The Reverend Alison Cheek with two supporters, at her irregular ordination in Philadelphia.

Memories flow back into her mind. Once, she recalls, there was no place to prepare for a mass and "I'd be vesting or divesting [dressing, undressing] in the ladies' room and a woman reporter would be in there with me, interviewing!" One of the women ordained with her was Carter Heyward, who inscribed the book she wrote about the incidents to her friend: "For Alison. To whom this book is really dedicated and without whom I personally could not have come along this far in our strange journey. Or so it seems to me, Sister, Oh, Sister. I love you. . . . On we go!"

Alison was ultimately accepted legally as priest, but her feelings toward the church hierarchy had dampened. She did not attempt to become a parish rector but continued her private psychotherapy practice. Bruce was then in the process of changing jobs, and the possibility loomed that she and her husband might move to Geneva, where he would take a position with the World Health Organization.

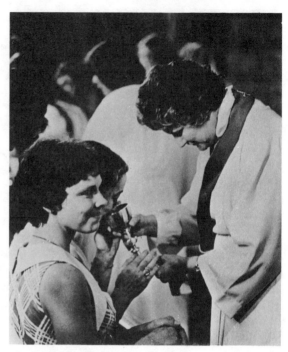

Cheek officiating at Communion.

In 1977 Bruce Cheek died. His then-fifty-year-old wife—he had called her Ali—says, "Before his death, I'd felt we'd achieved a kind of nice new balance in our marriage, after going through turmoil and rocky stuff. We were well through it—our troubles. I almost kind of fell in love with him all over again, with a different person. Not an image. I fell in love with a whole person." Their children had just left home, and the couple was experiencing "a different taste of life. A lovely fresh, new phase of life." She adds, "I felt terribly cheated when he died."

The door of her apartment still reads "Mr. and Mrs. Bruce Cheek," and on the antique piano is a photograph of her husband. It was in this apartment that Alison found Bruce, who had come home that day from work and died quietly while resting on his bed.

A big chocolate eater, he had removed a Hershey bar from his pocket and placed it on his dresser before he lay down. His wife, who chose to bury him in his favorite shirt, a red turtleneck, slipped the candy into his pocket before he was buried. Alison Cheek giggles at this pleasant memory. "He *loved* chocolate! I felt like some Egyptian sending the body off with pots, pans, food."

Prior to Bruce's death, she had finally achieved a second career, after her first one of bringing up children. Now she was being forced to face yet another change in her life. Says her daughter, "I can't see my mother living out the rest of her life alone. My father encouraged my mother to go out and do things on her own. He was there when needed. He was a compassionate person."

Alison "feels independent. I don't know how women who have never done anything with themselves manage" when a spouse dies.

Today the Reverend Cheek continues to practice as a pastoral psychotherapist. "I spend a large portion of my day journeying with people as they live out and struggle with their personal sagas, engaging in that tough and tender dialogue known as psychotherapy."

Her Washington office reflects her personality. It was the first place to be totally her own after going from her parents' house to her husband's, the place where she stood totally on her own two feet. It is filled with her belongings. "I put everything into it that I love." Decorations include a painting of Moses, a watercolor of the Adelaide hills "near where I grew up," a depiction of Tahiti, West African art, a scene of Spain, another of sheep shearers.

About her work she says simply, "I do love it." Her patients are not necessarily Episcopalians. "Sometimes they're scared that I'm going to lay a religious trip on them," she says, but they quickly get over that. Of psychotherapy: "It was entirely up to me whether I made it or blew it. I practice the art of psychotherapy with zest and delight."

Alison seems to know exactly where she has been and where

she is going. A woman friend says to her, "You're very percep-
tive." Cheek nods. "Yes, I am." And she looks at herself with
perspective: "My late blooming was really gradual. Just very very
gradual . . . until, before I knew it, I was there." Now comfortable
being in control, she feels one either looks at life, self-analyzes,
and acts as one grows older, or one stagnates.

An acquaintance says parishioners of Cheek's parish church,
where she and her family belong, are envious of her. " 'She went
out and did it, and I didn't' is the attitude," and she adds that
many parish people felt Alison should have stayed home, as "any
other self-respecting mother would." And not only did she do
something with her life, but it was a feat not attained by any
woman previously.

The Reverend Alison M. Cheek, MDiv, is not one to wear her
religion on her sleeve. She laughs when asked if she believes in
God, does not answer, but instead discusses Lent: "The Lent
before last, I said I was going to give up suffering for Lent." She
adds that she hasn't recently done anything about Lent, which,
she explains, is meant to put one closer in touch with one's
religion. "I've been on the front line!"

Alison Cheek's daughter admires her integrity, honesty: "What
my mother has done has obviously had an influence on me."

Cheek is never a devious woman. She's also not predictable.
Belly dancing at midday. Usually seen in a long hippie-like dress
with a rather lumpy bag over one shoulder. A firm handshake and
a broad smile. While driving to her office recently, she turned to
her companion and asked, "Do you have any objections to going
through the car wash? It's Ladies' Day on Tuesday and I can get
my car washed for only $1.75." She laughingly explains, "I play
both sides of the street."

How Alison Cheek Did It

1. Alison Cheek received her bachelor's degree prior to marriage
and the birth of her four children.

2. Moving from continent to continent, she made a home for her family as she raised her offspring.

3. She recognized her interest in her religion and was able, as her husband financially and spiritually supported her, to gain deeper knowledge and insight by attending a seminary.

4. She took courses during the hours her youngest was in kindergarten.

5. Cheek was awarded the master of divinity degree when her youngest child was eleven.

6. As she recognized that she wished to be ordained, her marriage was affected. Facing the problem, she and Bruce sought counseling. "We both changed a lot."

7. Without her career, Alison would have been devastated by her husband's death. The mother-widow-priest-counselor-feminist continues to practice her profession in Washington, D.C.

10

Innovation in Iowa

Marlene Harper—everybody calls her Marty—today runs a travel business utilizing a side door and a spare room in her Manchester, Iowa, home.

> *Excerpt from a Harper family Christmas newsletter, written by Marty Harper's husband, David:*
> MARTY—now age 45, became a grandmother in June and is still a travel agent. Took Dave to Jamaica but forgot to tell him not to drink the water so brought him home in a shoe box. . . . Keeps a messy house and office and doesn't brush her teeth. . . .

Marty's personable husband, David, recalls that up until six years ago, their life was a disaster, financially. "Finally, two or three years ago everything worked. And now there's plenty of money." He pauses, then continues: "When we moved my insurance office from our home, I thought, Now the phone's going to stop ringing and we can really live in this house. But the move didn't change a hell of a lot because the phone still rings. But now it's for *Marty.* I'll come home for lunch, but we really can't have lunch together because five out of six times a customer is here.

"But I don't resent any success that Marty might enjoy. I really don't. This thing with Marty started as a hobby. And I encouraged her. I pushed her. . . .

"We still really don't have the household I was looking for. But I think I have accepted the fact—about a year and a half ago— that what I was looking for really wasn't what Marty wanted. It was what *I* wanted. What she wants is there [he points to the section of the house where her travel business is located]. And that's fine.

"I think there's a lot of femininity that's been lost. But she's happy. And she has to be happy. I'm not that selfish a person. Although I would love to come home, have her pour a martini for me. I really would. I guess I'm a chauvinist. I don't know. I'm very confused frankly. I'm not unhappy and I don't think Marty's unhappy. But . . .

"It's a hard thing for me to even talk about. . . . I don't get as uptight as I used to about Marty working out there at night. I'm not resentful but I think we've created a monster as far as our life is concerned."

Marty Harper was born Marlene Smith in 1934, the only child of an Iowa salesman and his wife. Marty's father, eleven years older than his wife, was "very definitely" the boss of the family, according to his daughter. "I dearly love and enjoy both of my parents," says Marty as she flashes her great smile.

The trim-figured woman grew up in Waterloo, Iowa, with no thought of a future career other than to become a wife and mother. While she was a senior in high school, a teacher asked if she might be interested in working part time in a local travel agency. Marty accepted the position and continued on a full-time basis after her high school graduation, as she chose not to attend college. "I was not frantically looking for a man," the reason she says many of her friends sought higher education. "I stayed on at the travel agency because I enjoyed it."

Her social life was pleasant as well as she began to date David Harper, a classmate of hers. David's postgraduation plans included college. Gibes Marty, "We were thinking possibly of get-

The Harper family in their Manchester kitchen.

ting married some day, and there was no point in his being *that* much smarter than me," and she began attending college with him on a part-time basis, continuing to work at the travel agency.

The Korean War meant Dave's leaving college and entering the service; the couple married during his first leave, then moved to Texas. "And so I was retired," says Marty, who is affectionately called "Old Paint" by her husband. Few jobs were available for servicemen's wives in their tiny town, so she enjoyed staying home as a new wife, reading. After finishing the Bible, she started on Mickey Spillane's books.

After Dave's discharge, a daughter, Laurie, was born in 1955. The couple moved back to Iowa, to their hometown of Waterloo, and Dave again entered college while working part time, and Marty stayed home with the baby. When a job was offered to Dave in a retail credit establishment, he dropped out of college and accepted the position, and they moved to a small town, Manchester, Iowa.

Marty, home with her infant, thought that "as soon as Laurie started school, I would go back to work." However, their financial situation necessitated her finding a position sooner, while pregnant with their second child, Jeffrey. "I'd stayed home and cooked and washed and cleaned and coffeed with neighbors and heard all their trials and tribulations and it was enough." She was glad to begin working again.

When Jeffrey was three months old, Marty began her job in the special education department for a four-county school district as secretary to the director of special education. She stayed in this position until 1973, through four directors.

After twelve years of contributing to the family's finances, and tiring of the special education position and a particular boss, she considered her options. Her daughter was grown and Jeffrey was entering high school. She was thirty-nine. David, finally a successful insurance man, asked, "What would you *really* like to do?" Up until then, "The only job that I really enjoyed was the travel agency job." So Dave said to her, "Why don't you do that?" The two saw the need for a such an agency in Manchester, population 5,000. "No competition in town," noted Marty dryly.

She decided to speak with agency owners in other cities to gather background information and went back to Waterloo, to talk to travel people she had known years before. They did not remember her and "didn't seem to have much of an interest in me." Undaunted—she refused to allow herself to become discouraged—Marty visited a second agency, where the owner, Betty Wilson, considered, and stated, "I'd like to have you for an outside rep." Marty had no idea what that was.

"So I started." Her light laugh rings out, the smile involves every part of her face, and she tells her story, carefully enunciating, using few contractions. She pulls up a leg and slips it under her; this Iowa-born woman goes barefoot in the house. Her blue eyes actually twinkle as she adds, "If you don't use your mind in some way, it becomes dull."

Betty Wilson had just started her agency in a town forty-seven miles away and appointed Marty Harper as a travel representative

affiliated with an established agency. This was advantageous to
Marty, because the federally mandated financial requirements
necessary to begin an independent agency are significant.

As Marty's plans materialized, Dave Harper broke with the
Manchester firm he was working for and began his own business
at home, enclosing a porch and moving in desks for him and a
secretary, plus a file cabinet. Marty's travel service would be
offered through the newly formed Dave Harper Insurance
Agency, they decided.

Marty thought her business would consist of filling an occa-
sional need to visit a relative or answering a businessman's in-
quiry about a trip to Chicago. After all, she felt, how many Manchester, Iowa, citizens would be planning extensive travel? But as
soon as she began her service, businessmen and people from
surrounding areas—Clayton County, part of Buchanan County,
Jones County, parts of western Dubuque—became customers.

Marty ran about three ads a month in the local paper; the copy
read:

> Did you know that the Dave Harper Agency offers a travel
> service?

It was to be strictly a supplement, enhancing his business image.

Dave soon hired a second woman to work in his at-home one-
room office, and Marty moved her travel paperwork into a pas-
sageway of her home: "I'd go and sit on the floor and use the
hallway." Things became difficult when David's secretaries and
customers began to walk over her to use the bathroom. Dave
eventually added another small room abutting the enclosed
porch.

Finally the Dave Harper Insurance Agency purchased its own
building, and Dave, his secretaries, and their desks moved out of
the Harper home. Marty's business domain now consisted of the
converted porch with its outside door—which she used as an
entranceway to her office—and the added office room.

Business progressed to the point where her agency affiliation,

Betty Wilson Agency, hired extra help to handle the business Harper was sending. In fact Marty finds it difficult to remain at her present size and recognizes she must either set limits—which means turning away customers who want her to book them, for example, a motel for one night—or else hire help and grow. As her husband puts it, "She has three choices: She continues the way she is, small enough not to justify additional help, or she gets the hell out of it. Or else she gets someone to help her and starts advertising." It is no longer a hobby, states David.

She says she loves it. Harper's business is located in an area of Iowa where roads bisect rolling hills and John Deere tractors pull out of fields onto highways, go about an eighth of a mile, and climb onto the farmer's land on the other side of the road. Manchester is equal distances from the larger towns of Cedar Rapids, Waterloo, and Dubuque.

Travelers who are natives of Iowa are generally not worldly and sophisticated. Her affiliate, ex-New Yorker Betty Wilson, who has aked Marty in the past, "Where do you find these people?," finds some of their questions incredible. Marty has been queried on how to check in at an airport. Whether there is a bathroom on an airplane. How one knows it is the end of a trip. She explains that older people who have never flown "don't want to feel like idiots." She loves the people, the vacation planning. "People in this area amaze me. One of my first calls was to Bangor. Not Maine. Wales." It took her some time to figure out that there is no airport in Wales.

Harper finds honeymooners the most enjoyable customers. Often, when a couple wants a honeymoon trip to Jamaica, she admonishes them to consider their budget. "Ozarks instead. Honeymooners are time-consuming, strictly because they're such fun."

It is essential that she thoroughly read travel journals because "I'm sitting here in the middle of Iowa . . . not many sales reps stop by." None in fact. So on her own, this high school graduate trained herself to be a knowledgeable, articulate, worldly professional.

She is successful financially as well. At first, her branch office received a straight commission, then she switched to a salary-plus-commission arrangement that enabled her to take advantage of discounted travel offers available to full-time travel agency employees.

At the beginning about one customer a day would come in; today she grosses $175,000 a year. But, she emphasizes, she is working hard for it. "People call in the morning before I'm out of bed. People call in the evening after I'm asleep." The Harpers do not have a separate line for the travel agency business: "In a town this size people will call your house if you don't answer your business phone."

The local community seems enthusiastic about this service in their small town. David Harper credits Marty's success to the fact that she is a conscientious individual "who cares." She also enjoys. Marty acknowledges one of the reasons she loves her business is for the "fam"—short for familiarization—trip packages offered to travel agents to acquaint them with particular locales. When asked if she travels a great deal, she says, "My answer is 'No.' My family's answer is 'Yes.'" One of the first trips offered to her was to Hawaii, spouses included, for an all-inclusive $99 for one week. Dave claims he hates traveling. He was not going to go, Marty recalls, "and my husband thought I was weird, *sick,* to want to be by myself with people I didn't even know."

David: "Why would you want to go to Hawaii? And leave me?"

Marty: I'd give my eyeteeth to go to Hawaii. *Everybody* wants to go to Hawaii."

"When he saw I was serious," and that she meant to go without him if he wouldn't join her, "when he saw I was bound and determined to do this dumb thing, he decided to go along also. He dragged his feet. He was not unkindly about it. He still thought it was a dumb thing to do."

Since that first "fam" trip, Marty Harper has gone on Caribbean cruises, to Mexico for ten days (Dave did not go), and to a ten-day seminar in the United Kingdom sponsored by British Airways. And more. "It's interesting to be with other travel agents," a new breed of people for her, what she calls "posh-type people. There was myself—I'd never been abroad before. It was fantastic." Marty has traveled to Calloway Park in Georgia, Seattle, Aruba, New Orleans. Dave, a golfer, has gone along for several golf trips. In addition to her own wanderings, she has sent Iowans to Africa, the Orient, Europe, Hawaii, and Mexico. She also has speaking engagements at local clubs.

At home some friends are envious. They haven't gotten up and done something as she did. She is different. She feels "many would not like to give up their bridge, golf, social clubs." She's done nothing special, in her opinion, but can't think of anyone else who has changed her life in the way she has. She believes women often think, "Here I am—you've been waiting for me," and carry this attitude into the marketplace.

At forty-six she states, "I'm strong. I'm healthy. I figure if I want to do something badly, it can be done." She adds that she is conscientious "to a fault."

This conscientiousness—which has made her successful—causes problems. During the years she had to, "Dave's never liked the idea of my working full time," yet this business continues past 4:30. She runs in and out to start dinner, goes back and tries once again to call an airline that has been busy all day, for example. It surprised her to find that she is working harder than when she

Marty, with husband Dave, escorting a group of Iowans in the Caribbean (1977).

worked full time in an office. Yet she loves it—"or I wouldn't do it."

Service with a smile, and a bell-like laugh. Marty Harper's business started as a part-time service—a hobby that would help her husband's business as well—yet it can no longer be considered a pastime. Dave is considering occupying a second building and perhaps she'll move her office in there, sharing his secretaries to answer calls. Then "when I'm out, *I am out.*"

"I'm happy with today." And her witty husband, when pressed, stops wisecracking, and admits, "Whatever I've ever wanted to do, Old Paint's gone along. I find it hard to do the same for her. But I'm working on it."

Excerpts from a Harper family Christmas newsletter, written by Marty Harper's husband, David:

JEFF—now age 18 . . . became an uncle and later a godfather. Still operates his window washing business and takes pictures for the local paper, usually of sporting events. Is active in all sporting events and has picked up a couple of high school letters. Not a bad looking kid except for the big ears and the big feet.

DAVE—now age 46, became a grandfather and has a lot of extra loose skin to prove it. Besides being crotchety and ornery, his other good points include baby sitting skills second to none. Thinks changing a diaper every 14 hours is adequate and is teaching grandson baby profanity talk. Picked up several new swear words while fishing in Alaska last summer. Will not admit he contributes to a messy house.

GINGER—now 14 [the family mutt] will celebrate her 15th birthday in March and suffered a minor setback this year when she lost her hearing. Unfortunately, this is all she has lost as her male friends just keep showing up. Her eyesight is excellent also and she spends a lot of time reading dirty dog magazines. She reads lips, but looks only at what she wants to hear.

LAURIE O'LEARY [Marty and Dave's daughter]—now age 24, and Joe became the parents of Joshua David, missing ole

Dave's birthday by one day. No longer is employed and is now a full time mother. She and Josh keep a very messy house and both talk baby talk a lot.

MARTY—now age 45, New Year's Resolution is to wear her prescribed bifocals and not have a messy house. Took Dave on a Caribbean cruise, got mad at him when he kept making jokes about the Virgin Islands. Tried to lose him in San Juan, but the Puerto Ricans were too smart for that and took him back to the boat. Has given up trying to find the "snagproof pantyhose" and now wears Dave's socks. . . . Still traveling. . . .

Marty Harper, who received an attaché case as a present from her parents upon starting her travel business, was asked, if she could do anything she wished tomorrow, what would it be? Her answer: "Travel. Naturally."

How Marty Harper Did It

1. The Harper's financial situation finally allowed Marty—a working mother by necessity—to think about a career/hobby in terms of her interests and abilities.

2. There was no travel agency in Manchester, and Marty, having worked in a travel office during and after high school, knew she'd enjoy operating one.

3. She discussed her idea with people in the business, and one, impressed with Harper, suggested that Marty set up an adjunct office. For Marty, this was a financially advantageous arrangement.

4. At the same time, Dave Harper opened his own insurance office; the Harpers felt that travel assistance would be an excellent service for Dave's new agency to offer.

5. Marty kept overhead low by working out of her home as she built her clientele.

6. The concern and excellent service she offers her customers at times irritate her husband, yet have made her a success.

11

Little But Mighty

"Better to bloom late than not at all!" says Dorothy White, who married in 1943, became a wife and mother for the next quarter century and, it was presumed, for the rest of her life. Yet, in 1974, the fifty-four-year-old ex-Girl Scout Leader, volunteer, parent, and homemaker ran for the Delafield, Wisconsin, mayor's seat. And with no experience whatsoever, won.

And then, after two mayoralty terms, the woman went a step further: spunky Mrs. White, at sixty, has secured a position as Client Relations Coordinator for a civil/structural municipal engineering consulting firm.

Her parents would be surprised. Dorothy's father, a wholesale grocery salesman in Cedar Rapids, Iowa (population then: 75,000), and her at-home mother influenced their children subtly: "We wanted to please them. But I don't ever remember getting a lot of discipline," recalls Dorothy. Although neither parent graduated from high school, "They were well-educated people. Both very intelligent." Dorothy has a younger sister and a brother, an electrical engineer, six years younger.

Dorothy remembers her growing-up years as a series of pleasant happenings in a home where her parents "loved each other and we knew it." Her mother, a Campfire leader, was interested in her daughter's high school activities: dramatics, debating, National Honor Society membership, newspaper reporting, and the vice presidency of the Student Council. "Those were the days when a *boy* had to be president of the Student Council," says Dot, who graduated in 1938.

Two Sunday school teachers significantly influenced Dot when she was a teenager: "They were strong women. They were active. They were models. While I was growing up, I had a *lot* of outstanding women in my life. I was never made to feel that being a woman was second-class. Until recently. I never *realized* we were so downtrodden."

Equal rights were never considered by Dorothy when she enrolled in Coe College in Cedar Rapids (she suddenly bursts forth with an old college football cheer), paying her way through school by working as a salesclerk while she lived at home.

Serious relationships in college? "I had one that broke up, thank goodness." Then, speaking of herself and her husband, Bob: "We had one of those hot campus romances!" She had been dating another Bob as well, and at Christmas she received "a mushy card and a bouquet of yellow roses. Both 'From Bob.' And I didn't know who to thank for what!" Eventually she dropped the mushy-card Bob and continued to date Bob White, who liked flowers.

After graduation, with a degree in education, Dot taught speech and English for a year at an Iowa high school. "Teachers were not allowed to date"; she sneaked to the next town to see White, her fiancé.

Dorothy married Bob during World War II, and "I worked all through the war because I had to." For the money. "When we settled down after World War II, Bob wanted to be the provider and he didn't want me to work. He would let me substitute but he wouldn't let me get a full-time teaching job. . . . He would not *hear* of it."

After a number of years of marriage Dorothy and Bob decided to adopt a daughter, Wendy; Dot continued to be at home, now as a mother. "I feel as if I've had the best of two worlds. Because I did have the fun of being a kept woman, staying home. And I

A young Dot, premarriage.

enjoyed all of the things I did. I really resented Betty Friedan [in
the early sixties]. It made me angry that she was trying to make
me feel guilty for staying home and being a mother. I knew I was
doing many worthwhile things." Involved in the PTA and president of the area's American Association of University Women.
"Somebody had to do things for the kids. I had a Girl Scout
Troop," commencing when Wendy was in the sixth grade and
continuing into her daughter's high school years, as the troop
became Mariner Scouts. Dorothy sentimentally displays the
bracelet presented by her scouts—each charm has a significance
—upon the troop's disbanding.

"And I was teaching in Sunday school. I was not wasting my life; I didn't feel guilty. Maybe a person's full potential is to be a good wife and mother."

As Wendy grew up, Dorothy, on rare occasions, substituted. She still held no full-time job, because, according to her husband, "basically we felt—she felt—there should be someone there when Wendy came home." Even in high school? "It's preferable."

Twenty-seven-year-old Wendy concurs. Her mother's availability meant a great deal to her. "My mother pushed me into a lot of things that have since become hobbies. She pushed me into taking swimming lessons, piano. And now I have a degree in music. And I don't mean it in the negative sense. She *encouraged* me. She never insisted. She never forced me. I was made to think it was all for my own benefit." Rather the same relationship Dorothy had with her mother.

After listening to her large-boned, heavy daughter, Dot pushes up her glasses and says, "When Wendy went to college, I wanted a full-time teaching job. But then teachers were a dime a dozen and I couldn't get one." So she continued to substitute. And be home for her husband when he wanted her to be, when he was not traveling.

But unexpectedly the Whites' quiet, traditional life pattern changed. For the year her daughter was a senior in college, Dorothy White was elected mayor. The circumstances that led her into politics still make her smile with delight, like a real-life Mrs. Santa Claus: "I've always been self-assured." She knew she could do whatever she wished. But this small bundle of dynamite hadn't had an opportunity to display her attributes to the outside world, although close friends recognized the energy and enthusiasm.

The chance presented itself as civic problems plagued Delafield, a lakefront Wisconsin community of natural beauty in the heart of Waukesha County. Homeowners' associations formed, and Dorothy and her husband, concerned about their community, were active. Somewhat lethargic Robert White, for seven-

teen years the treasurer of Allis-Chalmers International, then
vice president of another large corporation, and now an officer
of the Foreign Credit Insurance Association, often stood and
spoke his mind. His wife, homemaker and mother, was also vocal
during these gatherings: "Well, I always cared. If they had a
hearing and I had something to say, I'd go in and say it." A
rabble-rouser. Bob White recalls one particular hearing where
his five-foot-tall wife, upon listening to high-powered expert testimony, rose and pointed out that exactly opposite information
had been presented by the same group six months before. "Dot
had taken the trouble to do the research on the original testimony." He laughs. "[The experts] folded up their portfolios."
End of hearing. "The public service committee really got a kick
out of it because they hadn't bothered to read the testimony
either. Dot made it sound as if [the experts] were against motherhood to want to [disagree with the townspeople]!"

Dot's common sense, her thoroughness, and her dedication
were noticed. One day there was a knock on the White door.
Dorothy welcomed a committee of three activist citizens, and led
them into her living room. Assuming they wished to ask her
husband to run for the position of mayor, she said, "I'll get Bob."

Their response: "We don't want to speak with him. We want
to talk to you." She was sympathetic to their concerns; she must
be their next $3,000-a-year mayor. Her reaction to their request:
"Oh, you're kidding!"

Bob walked into the room. The visitors explained their mis-
sion; he turned to his wife: "You should do it." The small woman
recalls in her surprisingly strong, sharp voice, "I was really dum-
founded. I said to Bob, 'Do you realize how many night meetings
this means?,' because he doesn't like to be home alone at night."
His answer: "You can do it. You've got the background." Dorothy muses: "I wouldn't have done it if he weren't in favor of it.
Because it could be too much of a strain on a marriage." But with
his endorsement, she accepted the challenge.

Wendy recalls her mother accepting the nomination. "It surprised me that she took them up on it. It didn't surprise me that they asked her." She again was shocked when her father agreed: "He's very much one for having Mom home in the evenings when he's here. He doesn't like to be alone. Dad allowed her to run for the city's good."

"I had no idea it was going to be as time-consuming as it was," says Dot, who, when drafted, was tutoring a homebound student three times a week and, "I just couldn't let him go." She continued the teaching through her election. "It was hard campaigning. I went through the menopause in the middle of the campaign!" Her loud cackling laughter erupts. She says it didn't affect her at all. "I thought, this sure knocks the old myth aside. You're supposedly not very rational during the change of life."

Her rather ambiguous "White is Right" slogan, her claims of "mature judgment," and her stated promise to be available were effective. "I campaigned on the proposition that I would be a full-time mayor and that's one reason why women are good in politics, because they do have more time to devote to it." White defeated her heretofore-unopposed male opponent. Asked how she felt by a Waukesha *Freeman* reporter, White effused, "Great —a little scared. It's a big responsibility with lots of problems."

Newsman: Did you think you'd win?

White: Yes, right always prevails. . . . Sex had nothing to do with it. I had only a couple of elderly men who said they couldn't vote for a woman.

White always answered queries directly, except those concerning her age: "I don't think it's relevant. What difference does it make if I'm forty-five or sixty-five? You can tell from my pictures I'm not a kid."

Her opponent had said women were too excitable. But Dorothy says that once she was mayor, "I think I was the least emotional person on the whole council. I made up my mind I would

Mayor Dot White, after presiding at her first Council meeting.

never descend to the level of ranting or raving." She has a temper, "but I don't lose it when I shouldn't." Instead she goes home and bangs doors.

Wearing skirts to meetings so the men wouldn't feel threatened, she continued her role as wife and housekeeper: "The first year I was mayor, Bob was upset about being alone so much." For years he traveled while she stayed home. Now the tables were turned. To solve the problem, they started to time trips to coincide, and "he finally adjusted." Her feeling is "you have to bend and change." What if you happen to have an inflexible husband? Her answer: "You either divorce or you live in tension." Bob

White was interviewed by Waukesha *Freeman* reporter Terry Lindt for an article called "Mayor's Husband Is His Own Man":

Their home life hasn't changed and Mrs. White still does the housekeeping chores ("I'm not very handy around the house," White said).

An example: An out-of-town guest, a family friend, and Wendy, who no longer lives at home, joined the Whites for a sumptuous meal prepared by Dot. Dot and her visitor abruptly left to attend Dot's sewage committee meeting. Wendy and family friend, also rushing to an appointment, transferred the table's contents to the kitchen and departed. Hours later Dot and her companion, returning to the White home, walked into a kitchenful of piled, soiled dishes and cutlery, with the leftover roast swimming in congealing gravy. Mrs. White to Mr. White in the living room: "Couldn't you have *even* put the meat away?" Silence from the direction of the overstuffed chair facing the television.

Of a generation in which husbands ignore unrefrigerated meat, and with a mentality that refuses to consider equal household responsibilities, Dot White sees her life in rosy tones and reiterates: "I've had the fun of staying home and being housewife, and enjoying Wendy as she was growing up. And *now!* I've always felt that women's lib means the liberty to choose."

After serving for two terms, Dot White is again a citizen. Her activities in her community continue and the townspeople's respect and admiration for the loud-voiced yet smooth and confident woman are apparent at a sewage meeting:

White firmly shakes hands with a tall, young, handsome politician, and, bending her neck back to look up at him, she bursts forth, "We made it!" referring to a recent successful political battle. Seating herself at the conference table—the only female except for a stenographer—White says to the elderly man on her right, referring to the group's just-announced federal grant, "We get some money and you show up, huh?"

Questions are addressed to White more often than to the chair, although he is an engineer, during this after-dinner meeting on land acquisition, connections, pump station locations.

All points White makes are well taken, sensible, down-to-earth. Her simple language rebuts legal-pedantese. Articulate, hotshot downtown attorneys eventually agree with her. But it takes some time. This woman keeps plugging away: "I *still* don't understand . . ." During discussions, her thoughts are asked for, listened to. They call out "Dottie, Dottie," these three-piece-suited silk-tied graduate-educated Milwaukee businessmen by day and concerned suburban residents at night. Dot, who loves the saying "A camel is what a horse would look like if it were put together by a committee," has a question. Answer: "That is mentioned later, darling." The corporate lawyer laughs good-naturedly at Dot's persistence. She is one of the few vocal commissioners. Sensibly dressed, unpainted short nails. Substantial body, chunky arms. Glasses under short gray bangs. Friendly, open, bubbling with laughter, a rosy-faced Methodist with influence in her Lutheran-Catholic community. Words fly back and forth: interceptor, effluent. White knows their meaning, she has information. She talks about municipal bonding, politics, bank notes. Her sharp laugh breaks out when least expected—it almost shocks. Septic fields, legal ramifications. On and on into the night . . .

While she was mayor, Dot's town adopted its first master zoning plan. Delafield also decided, under Mayor White, to spend more than it ever had before on the sewage system, almost single-handedly implemented by Dot. She dealt with the engineering firms: "I think women are tougher negotiators than men." It was Dorothy who knew the federal regulations: "I learned an awful

lot. I went to everything I could, to learn to do the job." Training
sessions, planning meetings, zoning seminars. "I did a lot of
reading. Bob was a help in many ways [his finance background].
And I'm not above calling people and asking for information.
. . . Also, the longer you live, the more background stuff you've
got stored up here. I do read newspapers front to back." While
campaigning she claimed she would solve the city's sewage problems. "I said I would do it ecologically when I became mayor."
And she did, although, according to Wendy, "There were times
when she took a lot of verbal abuse." Yet Dot handled it. "I
admire that," says her only child.

This woman who developed from a mother and wife into a
savvy politician and a self-trained engineering expert and continues in her traditional female roles as well is, says her daughter,
a perfectionist and an unusual person. "I don't think most
women would be the least bit interested in doing what she did."
An old family friend describes White: "An assertive and gutsy
individual. She makes mistakes then tries again." An optimist.
Dot: "I'll buy that. I am." According to Wendy, "She's always
been a vocal person." Dot says what she thinks, says Wendy, but
"tactfully." The family friend, almost a relative—a contemporary
of Wendy's—recalls that when she was a little girl and had her
tonsils removed, Dorothy brought a giant box, with gifts to be
opened at certain times each day. "Fingernail polish, comic book,
kaleidoscope . . . It's that quality about her that's unique. It's that
kind of generosity that's special."

When Dot vacated the mayor's position, she sought employment with a number of engineering firms. She says, "I always
assume when I'm interviewed that I'll get the job." They'd be
fools not to grab her. "Where else would they get anyone with
all this experience? And let's face it, they do need token women
on EPA [Environmental Protection Agency] projects. I have been
the token woman on a number of commissions. . . . Why should
it bother me? It's good experience I wouldn't have otherwise."

Her present position with an engineering corporation includes

utilizing her funding expertise. She is required to be knowledgeable about government regulations; when proposals are submit-
ted, White is sure they are correct. With public involvement her
forte, she often makes the first contact calls with communities,
attends their discussion groups and meetings. "I've gotten a
wonderful reception from the engineers," who are involved in
civil engineering projects in northern Wisconsin and upper Pe-
ninsula Michigan, as well as nationwide. Recently her company
was dealing with a solid-waste problem and she said to the engineers: "I'm sure you guys can design something that will be
ecologically sound. But the biggest problem is to get the people
convinced." They agreed. She loves working with engineers:
"Such rational people."

Dorothy White, a friendly open individual who doesn't speak
frivolously and answers the phone, "This is Dorothy White,"
believes "you can't be exposed to too many things. I think we are
the product of all the people we've known and all the things we've
ever done."

It's a little house at the end of the street in this lakeside community, and the woman who stands at the door is little, too. Little
and stout and fluffy-haired with an open smile. Inside the house
there is a wall of family pictures, and the cat is perched on the
davenport. Only one individual lives here now: Dorothy White.
Her daughter is a grown woman and moved away from home
several years ago. And shortly after Dorothy enthusiastically
began her new career with a consulting engineering firm, Bob
White left this wife of thirty-four years for a younger woman. "I
don't know what I would have done if I didn't have my job"; her
marriage breakup would have devastated her. "Yeah . . . It would
have been a lot harder. I have my ups and downs now," but she'll
go on. "I will. I have to."

She adds in a rare note of bitterness: "Husbands want to be the
sole center of attention—when they are around to be." Dorothy
talks about men keeping their wives in boxes, available when

wanted. She crawled out of her box when she became mayor, then engineering consultant.

"I'd never have been qualified for this engineering job if I'd not been the mayor. It's one of the good fallouts of my four years in office. I really am enjoying my job and I do have more freedom —being alone now—to do my job.

"I asked Bob once, 'If I hadn't been the mayor . . .' And he said he didn't think it had anything to do with it," the end of their marriage. Her husband, upon leaving, stated she is no longer the woman she was when he married her. True. She has grown. But she disagrees, "No, I was *always* like this, but I don't think Bob knew it. I was a hard worker. I remember in my high school yearbook they wrote next to my picture, 'Little but Mighty.' I've always been a leader and a doer."

Before the separation, before she knew her husband was in love with another woman, Dorothy talked about husbands' reactions to wives who, at an advanced age, begin a career: "It tells something about men's own self-images if they can have a woman who is successful in her own right and they can be proud of her. It shows that they're sure of themselves, their masculinity, and their self-worth. The ones who are jealous are . . ." She left the sentence unfinished, adding that her husband "finds me more interesting. I think he *is* very proud." It amused her "how quickly he makes known to his friends" her accomplishments. However there *were* complaints while she was mayor: He lamented that she was attending meetings two, three, or four nights a week. And he said, "Everywhere we go, politics is discussed. I get so tired of hearing about it!" It sounds like a wife chagrined with her husband's business associates' work-related conversations.

Dot White considers these predivorce comments. "I guess the election was a real turning point in my life. I'm a better person for having had that experience, not only intellectually but in sensitivity to other people. It also gave me a toughness I never had before. If one can take the barbs and slurs that are heaped on public officials, one can take almost anything life can dish out, including an unfaithful husband and divorce.

"Being mayor was a real growing experience and stretched me mentally beyond anything I had ever done before. I wish I had more time left in my life to do all the possible things out there, but on the other hand I'm lucky to be doing such exciting things now. Some women never do get to realize their full potential. . . .

"Better to bloom late than not at all!"

How Dorothy White Did It

1. Dot White made a home for her family and, according to daughter Wendy, was there when her child needed her.

2. Interested and active in community affairs, Dot often voiced a knowledgeable opinion.

3. When, in her fifties, she was asked to become a political candidate, she agreed.

4. Once she was elected, Mayor White worked at being an outstanding public servant. She attended seminars, enrolled in courses, read profusely. She also gleaned information from available experts.

5. To utilize her mayoralty experience, White—now a self-made expert on municipal sewage systems—applied for positions with engineering firms.

6. She always assumed, when interviewed, she would be hired. And she was.

7. As her marriage ended, optimistic Dorothy considered herself fortunate to have an exciting new career. "I wish I had more time . . . to do all the possible things out there . . ."

12

Saga of Three Sisters

Main Cast

Carmen Bailey: Born in 1932, the oldest of the Freeman girls; a wife and mother, now divorced. Her present occupation: goat farmer.

Oleda Baker: The middle sister. She married, had a son, became a high-fashion model at an unheard-of twenty-eight, divorced, retired, remarried, began a mail-order business, separated, had a one-woman art exhibit, wrote beauty books, reconciled with her husband, authored a novel.

Mary Frances (Francey) Petty: The baby in the ultra-religious Freeman home in Florida, born in 1943. Married a minister, shouldered the church-related responsibilities and activities, bore children, then began an architectural and interior decoration business, Francey Petty Designs.

Supporting Cast

Harry Freeman: The brother of three achieving Late Bloomers; personable, charming, and a felon—white-collar crimes only. Oleda with her droll wit: "You'll love him in half an hour, or maybe five minutes. Just don't trust him." Carmen says he's honest in his own crooked way. Married to a Baptist minister's daughter, Harry "wasn't allowed to be in the Boy Scouts," says Francey. "He didn't finish high school and left to go into the navy at seventeen."

Jack Bailey: Carmen's ex. A sophisticated good ole boy from North Carolina.

Stephen Baker: Husband to Oleda. Creative ad man and author.

James Petty: Francey's minister husband who oversees a flock of Church of Christ believers in a wealthy Fort Worth area.

Mr. Freeman: Handsome head of family; after preaching fire and brimstone to his fearful daughters and son, was caught in an act of adultery by his wife. Now married to a woman thirty-three years his junior, Freeman, at sixty-eight, wrote a report called "How to Have the Sexual Drive You've Always Dreamed Of."

Mrs. Freeman: At sixty-nine, her beauty—passed on to her children—is still apparent. Mrs. Freeman, who, says daughter Oleda, "never did anything . . . in her whole life except to raise her kids, keep house, and go to church," can't understand her daughters. She brought them up to become religious wives and mothers.

"I don't know why a woman would decide, 'Now is the time to do what I've always wanted to do.' And why three girls in the same family would do it puzzles me," says Carmen Bailey, eldest of the sisters. "I don't know why we sisters are all the same. We do know what we want. And we don't agree with the way we were reared; we go completely the other way."

No one is more surprised at these multiple turns of events than Carmen's, Oleda's, and Francey's parents, who raised their children in the Dade County, Florida, area of Allapattah. "It was a poor section," Oleda recalls. The Freeman children concur that their father was a strict parent and a hard worker. Francey's husband, a liberal minister, describes his father-in-law as "a George Wallace man"—and shudders.

As an auto mechanic who son-in-law Stephen Baker says is "certainly a genius mechanically," Freeman saved his money for years "to get us into the right environment," says Carmen. Mr. Freeman's parents had owned a Florida strawberry farm, and she found out a few years back that "Dad was at one time a farmer himself. He loved it but had to quit to make a living."

Although Carmen and her father have farming in common, "Dad and I didn't get along too good. We've never had much to say to each other."

The sisters have similar childhood recollections, with Francey, the baby of the family, remembering a somewhat less rigid life style. One refers to their home as a "morbid household"; another says their parents were "extremely harsh, neglectful."

"My father's favorite daughter?" Carmen says rhetorically. "Well *I* wasn't, that's for sure. I used to be pretty bitter toward Dad. He was rough on all of us—but in particular my brother, Harry, and me." Her mother was even harsher. "It was me that caught it. . . . And I didn't talk back. I would have had my teeth slapped down my throat. Or worse."

Mrs. Freeman admits she was a physically abusive parent. She spanked. "Yeah. Too much so. Like I was spanked. Like my mother did." She feels guilty about this; if given a second chance she would discipline differently. "I try not to let it get me down, you know. You can't live in the past. Mary Frances [Francey, the youngest] got very few spankings at all." Francey says her mother and grandmother "see it as 'raising our children in a Christian way so they won't be affected by evil influences.' " "I was very resentful," Carmen states.

"Carmen was a very difficult, selfish little girl," declares Mrs. Freeman. Oleda disagrees; she views her older sister as a victim and a particular episode illustrates Carmen's adolescent dilemma: Oleda wished to wear Carmen's blouse; Carmen refused to lend it. Oleda says, "I took that blouse and ripped it to pieces" when her mother was not home. When Mrs. Freeman returned, Carmen tearfully told her mother what her younger sister had done. Mrs. Freeman asked about the episode, and Oleda replied "in my sweetest, most innocent voice, 'No, mother. I didn't rip this blouse.' " Mrs. Freeman turned to Carmen: "If Oleda says she didn't rip this blouse, Oleda didn't rip this blouse." Mrs. Freeman has no memory of the incident but Oleda does. "And I never got punished for it." Her extraordinary prominent eyes blink once as she thinks, then adds, "No wonder Carmen's so angry!"

"Very rebellious, very rebellious," insists Mrs. Freeman. "Carmen had it in her mind we were trying to take her away from her friends," as the Freemans moved to the new big house in affluent Miami Shores after years of financial struggle. She shakes her head, and repeats: "Carmen was very rebellious." Oleda softens this judgment; her parents consider a one-time experiment with a cigarette as "very rebellious," she explains. In fact, Carmen was severely punished for just that. And since the incident took place on a glee club trip, Oleda, years later, was not allowed to travel with the singing group. Mrs. Freeman again admits she was strictest with Carmen: "You get more lenient as they come along . . . 'cause you see that it didn't work anyhow." But Carmen was a difficult child nonetheless: "She would not move her bowels in the toilet. She would *not*. And she was three and four years old." Mrs. Freeman's strong southern accent gets heavier as she remembers her determined little girl, while Oleda speaks softly of Carmen: "She was a frightened child."

The insecure young Carmen grew into a woman who today looks at her parents as "people who dealt with life as best they could. As an adult I see my father more as an individual with problems. I like him, but he's not the kind of person you love, who you are comfortable around."

Mr. Freeman did not express affection for any of his family members. Francey wanted "nothing more than to sit upon my father's knee, just once." And Francey and her husband do not recall Grandfather Freeman ever fondling his grandchildren, "except by accident."

He apparently did not fondle his wife either, who "devoted her life to her home and her kids even though she didn't know how to do that," says a daughter. Mrs. Freeman: "I spent my life cleaning that house."

Until her divorce.

Mr. Freeman believes the circle of the saved is small and he is in it. Yet after decades of preaching to his children to live in a Christian manner, he had difficulty following his own rules. Francey told her mother about Ellen, Freeman's mistress. "Mother wouldn't believe me" at first. According to the daughters, Ellen was not the first, and Church of Christ minister James Petty, Francey's husband, exclaims, "All the time he was a deacon in the church!" ("And my father is still *very* radical about church things," adds Francey. "He thinks Jim is a heretic!")

"I love Ellen," says Carmen, who was amazed at her father's infidelity. "And she's a Jew. Daddy *hates* Jews." Ellen, thirty-three years younger than Freeman, eventually married him. He now cares for his ill wife; the second Mrs. Freeman became a multiple sclerosis victim soon after the marriage. A daughter admits, "I like Ellen better than Daddy."

Less tolerant of his daughters' romances than his own, Freeman did not allow Francey to date, except once or twice, in high school. Even so, the Freeman parents were, by comparison, lenient with this daughter. "Mother saw some of her mistakes by then," says Oleda. "I think she was seeing what was happening to Carmen."

Carmen

"No dating, no going to movies, no dancing. 'Sit with your legs crossed, go to church.'" Carmen thinks about her teen years. "And when Jack came along, there was *no way* I could find a better Christian man than this one right here. I was permitted to date him." She adds, "I wanted to go to nursing school." But her parents nixed it. "I don't see how I was as dumb as I was. I was the dumbest one of the whole bunch of us kids. It took me longer to catch on, to figure things out. I was raised to get married and have babies. And iron. And that's what I did."

She married Jack Bailey, the son of her mother's friend, and the Baileys moved to Louisville, thirteen miles west of Winston-Salem, in North Carolina. "Too young. Eighteen. I was farmed out."

Carmen was a beautiful bride, not unusual in the Freeman family. Jack Bailey says, "The Freeman women come by their looks naturally. You ought to go down there [to Florida] and see her mother and her aunts. I declare that they're the most beautiful women in their sixties you could imagine."

Younger sister Francey says Carmen has "a much better brain, basically," than either herself or Oleda. Oleda agrees. Carmen is a self-taught pianist, guitarist, and violinist, but her childhood was filled with her mother's pronouncements that she was not a bright child; today Mrs. Freeman tardily admits Carmen is "very bright."

Carmen, a brown-eyed, tall woman, with a Jane Fonda smile, speaks in her Carolina accent mingled with Floridian undertones —a pleasing voice. She slowly recognized, after years of marriage and mental illness, that the vocation of wife and mother was not fulfilling, as her children grew older: "And I wanted to *feel* appreciated, not be *told* I was." Her husband considered her efforts and labors to be her duty as a Christian spouse and mother.

Jack Bailey was twenty-three when he married Carmen. After attending college for a couple of years—he wanted to be a preacher—he instead began building, selling, and investing in homes and property, successfully. "He's a genius," states Carmen, although he plays the country bumpkin, backwoods boy, chewing the fat about horse trades, smiling broadly. His deep southern laughter, heavy Carolina drawl, and apparently open demeanor almost mask his intelligence and knowledge. He is the son of a deeply religious couple, and his notions about marriage and the relative responsibilities of a wife and a husband were impossible for Carmen to live up to.

A childhood spent trying to satisfy her parents' desires fol-

Carmen Bailey, a young mother and wife, visited her New York City model-sister and had professional photos taken for fun.

lowed by adult attempts to please her husband. Finally, she gave up. Tired, despondent, depressed, and angry, after unsuccessful psychiatry, she became an advocate of proper nutrition and the importance of consuming organically grown foods. She began to grow her own food and found, as she followed this self-conceived regimen, that her mental anguish disappeared. "I started asserting myself, my feelings, my thoughts, my rights, and Jack began to say that I was aggressive, obstinate and hardheaded." Perhaps he was right. In her late forties, after years of being, she says, a subservient individual within the household, Carmen realized there was something else she wished to do. Farm.

"I can look back now and see that farming is what I always wanted to do, consciously, since the age of ten. But because girls shouldn't wear pants—they should want to type and sweep the floors and have babies—I repressed all those things and I had my babies and I fixed the meals and I washed the clothes and I gave my husband sex and I went to church. And I still wasn't happy. Jack expected to be listened to and I was raised that way too. To expect a man to be that way, and to honor him for being that way. And to cater to him, *help* him be like that. And little by little I saw I wasn't ready to meet my Maker that way."

She suggested she begin a goat and vegetable farm. "And Jack said, 'Oh no! You don't have time to do that today. You have to sweep the floor today, wash clothes.'"

Marital problems continued. Carmen moved with her two younger children—the two older had left home—from Winston-Salem to property Jack owned on the North Carolina coast, to think about her marriage in terms of her own needs. And she began to farm her South Port land.

"Did I tell you about my black neighbors, the Frinks, in South Port, who were looking out for me after the ground was first cleared? Mr. Frink told me, 'Now Miz Bailey, you can't expect much from land the first year. The soil is too acid, and lime takes too long to work to expect much this year.' So I made tons of compost, dug trenches with my rear-mounted rotary tiller, filled them with compost, and planted." The farmer-woman, who loves crossword puzzles and Chaucer, laughs. "I had *beautiful* large plants."

Farmers often feel the need to project a tough image when dealing with their animals. Female farmer Bailey treats her live-stock as if they were her children. "I have a mother instinct that won't quit. Maybe that's what my farming is all about, from plants to animals." She ministers to her livestock with herbs, garlic. And their robust health and large size indicate that they respond to this humane mothering: "I've got twenty-two goats, eleven of them kids. Four more kids are expected."

Living away from Jack was serene. She recalls a particular day with her boys—"Just the three of us having a ball. Jack comes

Farmer Bailey and baby goat: "I bottle-feed two kids because they can't find the dam's teats. Her udder is so huge it drags the floor. The kids look under her leg."
Photo by Jonathan Bailey

down there and says, 'Why don't you put a dress on and do something more ladylike?' " Jack Bailey, polite, gentle-seeming, charming, determined, stubborn, convinced his wife they should be back together again. She insisted she must have a farm wherever she was. They moved to King, North Carolina, near Greensboro, and the planting and animal raising was begun in earnest. Jack, who essentially retired from his own businesses, helped her as the farm became more self-sustaining.

Oleda's husband says, "Carmen's a little bit disappointed and frustrated as a person, because of what happened to her; her unhappiness had deep roots, back to her childhood, and dissatisfaction with her role within her parent-arranged marriage continued. And Jack, who tried to understand his wife, had his own upbringing and marital standards to contend with. He lacked the needed flexibility, or perhaps Carmen could not forgive him for her years of, in her mind, slave labor. "I think I knew what I wanted and I'd been waiting years to get it." She divorced her husband against his wishes. Although "I've never had money of my own" in spite of Jack's success, "I doubt I'll marry again. I'm already independent now. I'm willing to take my licks."

Hard-working, physically tough Carmen Bailey does not smile frequently. But her expressive face lights up regularly when she speaks of her at-home sons Jonathan (who was 1967 Regional Easter Seal Child) and Jesse. And her truck farm.

Her voice, low-key and strangely arresting while she talked of her married years, now becomes alive, enthusiastic. "I love it all." Mixing feed, breeding the goats, milking. Animal deliveries. "I love the farm, to dig in it, plow it. . . . I want to get a real heavy milk line. My greenhouse is full of seedlings. I've got about a hundred and eighty chickens. . . . It's tranquil and I cannot live in ugly or noisy surroundings. For me to know what a plant needs, for me to get it to grow, for me to serve it to the family, to make us feel good, or to sell it to people who need and want the same thing . . . it's a source of pride for me. To be as close to nature . . . " She has guinea hens to eat the bugs, Bantam roosters and hens, rare chickens. She grows okra, tender greens, swiss chard, mustard, spinach, summer squash, zucchini, three types of pumpkin, two types of watermelon, peppers, tomatoes, vegetable spaghetti, broccoli, cauliflower, cabbage, Hubbard squash, comfrey—which she uses medicinally—wormwood, strawberries. "I'm starting off on the small side."

Customers who want fertile and free-range eggs with the deep yellow yolks are willing to pay for them, she says as she walks toward the coop where the chickens feed on home-grown greens. Cider vinegar and kelp are given to the poultry along with yeast, "and then you get a wholesome egg." She feeds yeast to her children also. She talks calcium, magnesium, B_6, preaches organic farming with intelligence, after reading a tremendous amount about animal husbandry and crop-growing minerals "written for people like me—city folk who want to farm." She will talk at length on compost. Her desk is piled with animal books; prior to company's arrival, baby chicks were kept warm in the guest bedroom. The housekeeping is relaxed. So is Carmen, now.

She remembers meeting a couple when she was a child. "I don't recall their names. I was eleven years old. I asked the lady how she could be so contented, so calm. *I* never felt that way. It seemed to me that people who were happy didn't have myriads of rules to live by. And I'm just now getting it all together enough to do the same."

The ex-wife who was concerned about dressing like a lady for her husband now loves trudging about in torn tennis shoes and dungarees and is beautiful in them. At her special quiet place down by her creek, she sits, cigarette in hand, and thinks about her upbringing, her marriage, and the raising of four children, the future. And practical matters. "To do what I want to do, I've got to be organized. That means the kiddies eat breakfast before it's time to let the chickens out and fed. Then I can get over and feed the goats. . . ." She's up at six, carrying in a milk can of goat colostrum to the freezer, and her day ends long after she serves her boys country ham, and biscuits made of blends of brown rice, raw and toasted soy flour, toasted carob flour. Fresh-picked greens, homemade pumpkin pie topped with yogurt. "Every ounce of creative talent I have is used on the farm, a blend of everything I love. Putting the garden here this year and the melons over there and making it all look pretty." A challenge. "I love doing farm work, it is a source of pride that I can. And I'm not skilled for a specific job if I wanted one. The farm fills that need. I'm doing exactly what fits." (And, says Oleda, "If Carmen tells you something, you can buy it.")

Their mother, Thelma Freeman, is confused. "I just don't

On the North Carolina farm, hard physical labor and new beginnings for Carmen.
Photos by Jonathan Bailey

understand. These things that my daughters do never *entered* my mind. I just thought they'd get married and have a home, you know. Raise children. It was just logical to think that, you know. That's all I had done, you know."

Carmen Bailey sits on her living room sofa under an Oleda primitive painting hung on the wall's ten-inch-wide logs, horizontally sandwiching three-inch-thick mortar, as Jesse and Jonathan bound in, chattering in a thick Carolina twang. Carmen, touching and affectionate with her children, whisks them into the kitchen for after-school homemade yogurt and honey. Walking back to the sofa, she echoes sister Francey: "I would have loved for my Daddy to put me on his lap just one time *at least.* He never did." Then her mind turns to her closest sister in age: "Oleda is astute and, as Jack puts it, makes every edge cut. She's an opportunist and that's a plus for her. I'm the opposite. I think it's clever of Oleda to do what she did, and sharp of me to recognize what I need and want." Tranquillity.

Oleda

Tranquillity is not Oleda Freeman Baker's long suit. Creating, producing, deciding, moving, doing: these are the terms of her life after much the same childhood as Carmen. But with important differences.

"My mother thought I was so perfect when I was fourteen, fifteen years old," Oleda speaks in her careful and strong, almost loud, yet surprisingly feminine voice, soothing to hear. A sister comments that today Mr. Freeman "eats out of Oleda's hand because she is financially successful, which . . . means an awful lot to men." Oleda and Carmen continue to evoke diverse responses from their parents as Carmen works toward her goals in a quiet, straightforward manner. Oleda has a different style.

At forty-five this beauty-products corporation owner, controlling over a million dollars annually, writes novels, is an artist, and is forming a women's wear business. But in proverbial success-story manner, life did not start out that way. Born two years after Carmen into the church-centered Freeman home, Oleda was a poor-to-average student at Miami Edison High, where she was "much too shy to be a cheerleader. I walked down the hall looking at the floor." Carmen concurs: "Shy as a child, embarrassingly so, painfully so. She was glum-looking. Didn't talk much." Aware that she had a problem, Oleda forced herself to sign up for dramatics in the fall of her sophomore year. "And I was practically throwing up all summer . . . thinking, 'How could I do that?' " She decided to try directing instead during her junior and senior years.

When chosen as a senior calendar model, Oleda was surprised. "I thought I was terrible-looking. I did think I had nice eyes and good hair." Carmen says her sister "had lousy posture as a kid." But Oleda was concerned about her appearance. "She used to make me so mad; she was so prissy and would sit up late at night fussing with her face."

The beautifully made up Oleda remembers being allowed to date one boy "when I was in the tenth grade." A member of the church, "he could only take me to the church's young people's class, have an ice cream, then take me right home." The time necessary for the class and ice cream plus travel was computed by her parents. Those exophthalmic eyes, holding a perpetual look of surprise, widen: "The boys I dated were as square as I was." Necking had no place in Oleda's teen years.

"When I got out of high school I stayed home, just helping my mother." There was no plan for a career, no thought of college. "I was raised to be a wife and a mother and the right guy didn't come along and I was just sitting there. Waiting.

"And then being engaged and unengaged and engaged again . . . I kept changing my mind." Younger sister Francey says Oleda, feminine, demure, "broke a lot of hearts." According to Oleda, the fiancés were "substantial and nice and polite and had good manners. But I had no idea what I wanted, or what I

Oleda represented the month of May in her high school calendar.

needed." When asked how many engagements she ended, the mammoth eyes ringed with unbelievable eyelashes sparkle with merriment. "I'd have to think about it." More than five? "Probably . . . Yes." (Her mother recalls covering up for Oleda, who would forgetfully make two dates for the same evening.)

So Oleda continued to wait for Prince Charming until a family friend told Mr. and Mrs. Freeman: "Look, you should let your daughter work!"

She got a job at Burdine's, a Florida department store chain, where, as a clerk, the unconventional beauty was asked to model for the store. Excited, Oleda discussed it with her parents.

No daughter of theirs was going to be a model. They were adamant. She went back to work the next day and refused the modeling position; it never entered her mind to argue.

After Burdine's, she worked at the telephone company. And met David Pettis. Different from the church boys, Pettis seemed deeper, older: "He had been around a lot more. He was the first man I was involved with in a sexual way." She had been taught that the individual you have sexual relations with is your spouse; she was almost twenty-two when they wed.

Married for two years, Oleda, remembering the Burdine's offer, yearned to be a model. Her husband agreed to allow her to attend modeling school: "At that time he *let* me go. That's the way it was."

Her face and figure propelled her into modeling assignments in southeastern Florida. After their baby, David, Jr., was born,

Mr. and Mrs. David Pettis, at their Florida wedding.

Oleda lost the weight gained during the pregnancy before she left the hospital and continued modeling. "I was the only high-fashion model they had, practically," remembers Oleda of her Miami career. However, the modeling capital is New York City; Florida is small-time.

Although "I was chicken," her husband encouraged her to go north, leaving their toddler with David's paternal grandmother.

Oleda was an unheard-of twenty-six as she traveled to New York City to begin her high-fashion modeling career. "That's late. You really must start when you're in your teens." Within six weeks, she was posing for *Vogue* magazine, and "my husband asked for the transfer he said he would if I were successful. . . . Within two months we were all together again."

Oleda Baker, a come-lately Manhattan model.

Even before her move to New York, there was a strain on the marriage: "I started growing so fast after I left my mother's house." She had been married for some five years, and New York whetted her rapidly maturing appetite for living. "I realized how different I and my husband were, and people that I grew up with down South were, from the people in New York. The things they thought about, the things they were involved in . . ."

Pettis embarrassed her by circulating her fashion photos at social events, speaking only of his wife's success, for there was little else in his life, she says. Oleda outgrew him and soon asked for a divorce. She did not ask for alimony or child support. "My point was, I'll do it myself. Just end it and move on." Pettis went to pieces "because he really did love us" and removed from their joint banking account the money Oleda had planned to use to establish herself; he hoped to make her come back home to Florida with him.

"But I just started over," and within months she was successful enough to hire a live-in housekeeper to care for her child. The late-blooming model continued to work in the field for thirteen years. "I was the oldest model around" who still played the young woman, not modeling as an older woman.

And she began to date. "I did the whole social circle. But I knew what I wanted." Stephen Baker.

She found him in a smoke-filled room packed with drinking, talking, laughing, partying sophisticates. The photographer-host met her at the door. "He introduced me to Steve. My husband."

It is hard to get a grip on Stephen Baker's character, to be able to feel one knows this man, who describes his first meeting with Oleda in his deep, heavy monotone voice overlying a Hungarian accent: "How could I forget? It was a models' party thrown by a photographer. Ninety-nine percent models show up [at this sort of gathering], and the men are clients. The idea is to show the men a good time. . . . There were so many beautiful women there and so many drunk men. There was no organized pairing off. Everyone was dancing. I went through just about every model there was, with mixed success. It was a very slow process. . . . At that time I had some fixed ideas about models. I thought they all came out of the same mold. I didn't think very much of them intellectually. Mind you, I was an art director and I had associated with models for years.

"And Oleda surprised me." Excited about his newest book, he was anxious to talk about it. None of the models would listen. "But Oleda asked some intelligent questions. And they were relevant questions, which indicated to me that she was listening.

"I thought she was refreshing, honest, and very straightfor-

Oleda and her spouse, Stephen Baker, described by sister-in-law Francey as "virile-looking. Macho." **Photo by Barry Evans**

ward. I don't think she was naïve in a bad sense. She cut through much of the bullshit. I found her genuine. Very real. She was curious about what was going on. An excellent listener. That's what stands out in my mind. She was different than most of the women I knew because there was less veneer. She expressed her feelings, and there was no doubt in my mind that she felt the way she indicated. She wasn't putting on anything."

Thirteen years her senior, the Hungarian-born Baker was getting divorced himself. They met just for lunch for many weeks, eager to see each other. "I kept wanting to talk with him. He was foreign to me and I was foreign to him." They graduated in about a month to cocktails.

"We dated for four months before I ever slept with him. . . . That didn't always happen. I've dated other guys and gone to bed the first, well, maybe the third night I met them." (She adds jokingly, "I always like to know them *somewhat.* ")

Oleda's ex-husband had left for Florida, but Baker did not end his marriage as easily. His wife-related problems began to affect their relationship, Oleda recalls. "I have a way of putting things in boxes and if it doesn't work out in that box, you get rid of the whole box and move on to something else. Modeling never meant that much to me anyway," so she left New York and Stephen for Philadelphia, where her sister, Francey, was living.

Oleda stayed in Pennsylvania a short time, but long enough to become engaged to another man. "I sound terrible. It sounds like I have all these men following me and I just . . . But I'm not that way when I'm going with them. I care." She was infatuated and she liked and needed the new man. Stephen, with his divorce difficulties, had not been attentive and he says Oleda "is not a gambler. She likes a sure thing."

Steve called and called while she was away, but "I wouldn't come to the phone."

When Baker drove to Philadelphia a second time—after she refused to see him on his first trip—he convinced her to postpone her wedding for two weeks. During that time he promised to settle his divorce. Oleda went to her fiancé and called the marriage off permanently, but did not tell Stephen her marriage plans were dead: "Steve thought he had a two-week grace period only." And straightened out his problems.

Back in New York City Oleda and Stephen began living together as she modeled. Oleda does not remember the year they married, or her age. "I think it was 1965 or '67 or '68. I live in the future. I move on. I cannot keep up with my past. It's like a waste to remember."

They married in 1967 when Oleda was thirty-three, according to Steve, and his artistic, intelligent, creative wife, old to be modeling, eventually tired of it as well. Her husband, an author and the ad man responsible for the telephone company's "Let your fingers do the walking," told, in his 1979 book, *The Systematic Approach to Creativity,* of Oleda's metamorphosis:

> Weary of her modeling career, Oleda Baker . . . made a resolution on her fortieth birthday: to find a new career. She wanted one that would offer her both intellectual stimulation and financial rewards.
>
> A period of intensive soul searching came first. Oleda was sowing her creative oats to discover what would best satisfy her desires. She tried her hand at (a) designing jewelry, (b) making decoupage boxes, and (c), undaunted by her lack of formal art training, painting in oils. None of these experiments seemed to give her the fulfillment she was looking for; she wanted something uniquely her own.

And Oleda Baker again knew what she wanted. "I always know what I want.

"One of the biggest mistakes people make is saying, 'It can't be done' or, 'I don't know how' or, 'It's too big for me to handle.' You just *do* it. You see the end of the road and you head right to it. I was looking for something creative, after modeling. I don't want to sound pompous because I recommend it for any girl who wants to get doors opened. It teaches you poise. There are a lot of opportunities, you meet a lot of people . . . ." Models are accepted, no matter what their background. "So you have a choice of many careers."

Her first business experiment was with a friend; together they designed unisex jewelry for boutiques. Then she tried hand-manufacturing black and white Beardsley decoupage boxes. "And Bloomingdale's bought them! But I was making them all by hand. It was okay the first time around. But then, when they wanted a slew of them—they were selling them from twenty-five dollars to thirty-five dollars—I decided, 'This is ridiculous.' Once I start heading in a direction it takes me time to get with it. But once I do, I learn fast. I soon learned that what I did not want to do to become successful was all this hand labor myself. I just couldn't make enough money that way." She laughs. "And besides it was ruining my fingernails.

"I find the application first, then I work backwards. Get the idea, decide whether it's a marketable idea—*then* I worry about how I do it. And I just do it. So I tried all these different little things and decided anything I do on a one-to-one basis is just not going to make anything."

So she decided to write a book, "because you write one book and you sell a lot of them. . . . I used modeling as a stepping stone to get into writing because I wasn't a writer." Married to a creative ex-advertising agency head, and a writer—Baker is also the author of *How to Live with Your Neurotic Dog* and publications ranging from novels to golf books—Oleda told him she wished to write a beauty book and needed contacts. Stephen was not receptive. "He probably thought I couldn't do it on my own." He helped Oleda write a proposal, find a ghost writer, and obtain a contract. The book was titled *The Model's Way to Beauty, Slenderness, and Glowing Health.* "I was trying to get my own identity, and it was like he was the big father and I was the little girl. I was helpless and he had to tell me everything. I said, 'Steve, you know I really learn fast and I can handle some of this. Let me in on some of this. I have a lot more to say.' We had a lot of fights about that." In his own book on creativity, Stephen describes Oleda's book's conception:

> The idea for a book . . . occurred to Oleda after many months of trial and error. Intrigued by the subject of the book, the publisher agreed to a contract after seeing a one-page outline. Since this was Oleda's first attempt at book writing, she enlisted writer Bill Gale and photographer Richard Hochman to help her with the assignment.
>
> An extensive direct-response campaign helped boost book sales. In its first year, Model's Way sold more than 150,000 copies. Encouraged by the response, Oleda now felt that she was on her way to positioning herself in the marketplace as a beauty expert. Still, something was missing; there were other women like her who were capitalizing on their good looks.

Oleda recalls, "I wasn't even speaking to Steve at this point. And I decided I was going to get a contract on my own." She wrote an outline for a second book and would not let him read it. "And would you believe I got a contract?" Delighted laughter. Carmen describes Oleda as "a real competitor," and Carmen's ex-husband, Jack Bailey, sees this same will in the three sisters: "It goes back to Pop Freeman. They've quite a determination that won't quit. Stay right on it and stay right on it. Persistence. I see a lot of pushing other things aside. Freeman girls pick a narrow interest and when they get on that thing, that's what they're gonna do."

Oleda was thrilled with her literary success, but her problems with her husband were deepening. When he asked her to join him in California for three days, she refused, and while he was on the West Coast, moved out of their apartment. If she had told him her plans "he literally wouldn't let me out the door, would physically prevent me from leaving.

"I wanted to be a woman at home and a person at business. I

wanted him to protect me and take care of me. I'm strong but I don't always want to have to be strong. I want to feel that protective arm sometimes." Carmen says, "Oleda likes to lean on a man who is tall, strong, and handsome. But only up to a point." It's understandable that Stephen had trouble dealing with the beautiful, feminine, stately woman with an independent business mind. She looks so feminine, in need of protection. A delusion.

"You see, I loved my husband but there were a lot of problems. Although he *allowed me* to go my own way and do my own thing, on one hand he wanted me to and on one hand he didn't want me to. . . . And I really had to get out. I made it a point to not even consult him about anything. If I made a mistake, I made a mistake."

It was the Philadelphia experience all over again. She refused to speak with Steve. Settled into her apartment, with her son David in Florida with his father, "I dated men from out of town who were married," to avoid relationships where males would try to tell her what to do. She had one interest: "My goal was to be successful and make money." She put all her energies to that task.

Stephen tells about it:

Two other books, put together with the assistance of a secretary, were published soon after the first. Combined sales of *The I Hate to Makeup Book* and *Be a Woman* exceeded 250,000 copies. Oleda's innate marketing savvy was now beginning to pay off. She recognized that she had found a unique selling point in a crowded marketplace, one few other beauty experts could fill, that is, a very youthful appearance at 40-plus. Both in advertising and in her publicity stories, she decided that giving away her age (in years, months, and days) was more practical than it was painful.

Her present partner, Gene Schwartz, who, incredibly, says, "There is a great deal of innocence in the woman—Oleda's a young soul," bought one of her book's mail-order rights from the publisher and contacted Oleda about photos for advertising. She insisted on seeing the mail-order ad copy. A picture alone was not persuasive, in her opinion. She insisted her age—forty-one at the time—be added.

Mail-order sales were excellent, but Oleda slowly decided book writing "wasn't good enough any more. I decided—this was probably the most important decision in my life—that it's not enough to do something that sells, even if you sell a billion of them. It's not the way to go; you have to sell something that has [she pauses dramatically] *reorder possibilities!*" She laughs. (Brother-in-law Jim feels "a deprived childhood calls out for millions," and talks of "her desire to control." And his wife Francey, who feels Oleda is "tougher" than Carmen, says, "Oleda has changed drastically in the past fifteen years.")

Oleda had an idea. Impressed with the healing benefits of a vitamin A&D ointment, Oleda sent a tube to a chemical analysis laboratory. "I'd never done any of this before. I knew A and D are the only two vitamins that actually penetrate the skin," and, by adding ingredients to these vitamins, she, with the help of Gene Schwartz, by now her partner, put the first Oleda, Unlimited product on the market. The ad message—much like Schwartz's mail-order for Oleda's earlier books—is essentially unchanged today (see the ad on the next page).

"That's really been the pitch of my business. My age versus the pictures." And it's been an immensely successful campaign. She explains that "the customer orders it, they like it, they have to keep buying more and more. And now I'm into the vitamin business. They like my vitamin, it does well for them, they've got to buy one bottle every month. They like my creams; they've got to keep buying them. It's absolutely fantastic!" She finds the business of making money creative and stimulating. Stephen Baker narrates her success:

Other projects followed: a monthly column in Model's Circle, booklets on beauty tips (Oleda Baker's Face-Savers

and Oleda Baker's Hair Savers"), Confidential Reports on the Age-Less Diet, a series of TV minilectures on beauty and health, and finally a line of sixteen new beauty products promoted through an "age-less" catalog. Oleda's slogan is "Every Woman Has the Right to Be Beautiful!"

To Oleda's way of thinking, every woman has the opportunity to be successful and can develop the drive. She—along with her two sisters—does not accept helplessness. She remembers riding her older sister's too-large bike to school and having to push it most of the way. But she never mentioned it to her parents. The theory around the house was "I'll handle it and if I don't know how, I'll learn." This mentality causes her to be impatient with "so-called helpless people." "Do it yesterday" is a slogan of Oleda's—she feels you can't keep talking about something to be successful. "You have to *do* it. You have to have several prospects going at the same time so you aren't stopped if one thing falls through." She speaks with few catechisms, and her mellow voice is never shrill as she enunciates precisely, the voice of a self-educated, cultured woman who believes that women must create their own enthusiasm. "If someone is down and bored all the time, they aren't going to have the energy to do anything innovative. Energy makes energy. Excitement, interest makes energy. Part of it is psychological; part of it is health." And an individual does not have to be an expert in the field they're going into. "There are ways of getting around that"; streetsmarts are more important.

The streetwise world of Oleda Baker is classy, alive, expensive. Her main offices are on Lexington Avenue, but the place of business where she actually works is in the same building as her Tudor City Place apartment in Manhattan.

As she sits behind her fruitwood desk, she looks down at the new labels her cosmetic products will soon carry, a plan for a line of clothing color-coded with tags for women with specific figure problems, and piles of papers next to the covered crystal dish full

Businesswoman Baker (seated) in her Manhattan offices, where the atmosphere is pure femininity. **Photo by Barry Evans**

of pistachio nuts. This woman who has appeared in ads for Clairol, Revlon, and Elizabeth Arden, lightly pushing at her hair to give it height, says matter-of-factly, "I have very good hair," and creatively uses this fact to make money.

All Oleda, Unlimited activities go through her hands. Her cosmetics catalogue contains personal homilies among the creams, lipsticks, mascara:

> I'd like to introduce you to my "Age-Less" World that will liberate you at last from having to rely exclusively on Mother Nature. Because she has been known to fail us far too often—and far too frequently as we grow older. . . .
>
> When I turned 30, and I began seeing the first horrendous wrinkles creep across my face, I decided to fight them as though my entire future career depended upon it. Which it did. Just as your career—as a wife or lover—depends on it too. . . .

Yes, I have wrinkles at 43 years of age—but YOU can't see them . . . because I simply smooth them almost out of sight, every night when I go to bed. . . .

I lived my first 26 years in the sunny South. So I had to learn long ago how to get a tan without aging my skin. . . .

Think about this for a moment: if I were going to tell you that I could help you keep your body as young-looking as I keep mine (my so-called "vital measurements" are 34-23-35), then I'd have to give you a series of exercises that would take 30 minutes to an hour each day. In other words, to make your body younger-looking, you have to work. But to make your face younger-looking, my way, you just about don't have to do a thing. There's no work involved at all. Read how, on this page. (Incidentally, these unretouched photos were taken when I was exactly 43 years and 25 days old.) . . .

It's okay just to take a second and put a little lipstick on sometimes—but if you are going someplace special, wear your lipstick as if you were a movie star—after all—you *are* a star, so act like one! . . .

As far as I'm concerned, I'd rather be caught nude on Fifth Avenue than be caught without my eyelashes. I even sleep with mine on. . . .

Now other women can look at me, and excuse their own appearance by saying that I was "born lucky" as far as keeping my face and figure trim and young (which is not at all true, incidentally). But when they realize that I have been a two-process blonde for over 20 years—that I both bleach and color my hair—and my hair STILL looks like this . . . then they KNOW that I've discovered something that can work for THEM too. (And that may, incidentally, give them some of the most romantic moments of their life.) . . .

This is my long-time friend (and Executive Vice President of my company) Vernice. She, too, lives by "my" rules with make-up and skin care. Don't tell her I told you, but she is the same age I am. . . .

I hope you will believe what I have always told my son David—that is, you can do anything you really want to do —as long as you believe in yourself—(including looking fantastic). . . . I first started believing in myself at age 13— thank God for that! . . .

My husband Steve . . . tells me, I'm glad you try to keep yourself together for me. But what he doesn't know is that I do it for myself as much as for him—(*now*—he knows!). . . .

Baker says he never woke up in the morning and found that Oleda didn't look beautiful. Was she wearing makeup? "I'm not sure." He tells of once searching for a false eyelash in his chest hair.

With her wrinkle-free forehead, prominent cheekbones, and bluntly shaped long nails, she admits she tires of people saying she *couldn't* be forty-four years old, then adds, "When they stop saying that, I know I'm going to be worried!"

Her office walls are covered with her decoupage, made of photographs of her family and placed over doilies. A Persian painting hangs on the pale mustard wall. A delicate breakfront in salmon sits in one corner. The office sofa, covered with pillows and soft sculpture, faces Oleda's delicate desk, and the impression is of beauty and wealth.

Her storybook existence is in fact becoming a book. Putnam's is publishing her novel, *Reluctant Goddess,* about a young woman's rise in the cosmetics industry and based loosely upon her life. Her own castle, her own chauffeur, horse, car, businesses. And Dame Oleda Baker of Honor. The tale of a woman with a face, figure, and mind that insecure women—and men—would hate. (A male acquaintance says, "I have trouble with beauty queens. I think she's gorgeous to look at but I couldn't imagine messing up her hair.") Oleda's novel is the story of a strikingly handsome female who wants to be appreciated for her mind, her creativity, the unusual wife who loves her man but has found matrimony difficult.

An important part of Oleda's business responsibilities includes posing for photos used in her catalogs and ads. A well-controlled businesswoman, she doesn't, according to an ex-employee, "rant or rave. In business she is one clever woman." And a male business associate finds her demanding, "but reasonably so." Oleda's opinion: "There is no limit as to how I'll find out what I need to know." Photo by Barry Evans

During the several years of separation from Steve, Oleda wrote, organized her cosmetics mail-order business, and sold this first novel, receiving an incredible $37,500 advance on royalties. In December of 1977 Oleda and Stephen, still in love, felt they could rectify their difficulties and began living together again as husband and wife.

"Every marriage goes through phases," Steve Baker says. "What happens is that people develop in new directions and sometimes it is difficult for the other person to catch up." Oleda feels her husband now accepts her professional life and acknowledges her business acumen. "Now I can definitely say that he wants me to succeed."

She already has. With her graceful mannerisms and stoic look —one of her booklets advises against facial expressions because they cause wrinkles—Oleda Baker has beauty plus brains—what brother-in-law Jim describes as "a visual charisma"—and the sense to use them. A self-assured individual, this woman feels a satisfaction within her own life that allows her to be a forthright and outgoing individual.

A male publishing executive stares at her over a gourmet luncheon and asks, "How have you survived in the world of business, still being very sweet and very loyal?" The expected bitchy personality of the gorgeous glamour girl is not evident in Oleda Baker, although an old friend and business associate says that as a businesswoman Oleda is "hard." Women—if they get over envying her looks and her brains—like her as a human being. It's difficult not to. Her partner, Gene Schwartz, feels Oleda has a "cursed gift." In staccato, through his Jimmy Carter smile, he explains that beauty is a tremendous barrier, even for a woman: "People project a tremendous amount of stereotypes on Oleda, and the most comfortable stereotype is that she has no brains at all. And she's lived with that all her life. . . . Yet she assumed her true identity at the age of thirty-nine as she began to manifest her brains outwardly, through the writing of her books, the starting of the business, the *blossoming* of her own conceptions."

Vernice Gabriel, who met Oleda years ago when they were both represented by the same modeling agency, explains that Oleda is constantly living down her modeling background. "A model is not that enterprising. She's self-employed but it's all hinging on jobs here and there, and she doesn't have to use her mind. . . . So Oleda is proving—constantly—to men, 'I am good. I am smart. I am intelligent. I can be successful.' Because the men in her life have constantly made her prove it."

Once when Oleda and her husband argued, Stephen Baker

Sharp-thinking Oleda poses with her twenty-year-old son to accentuate her youthful appearance. In common with other Late Bloomers, she says her child "is one of the most important achievements of my life. I not only love him—I like him. He's an absolute delight."

took a card and glued a picture of Oleda onto it with words flowing from her:

> Hi. I am unlimited. I am a brain, not just a body. . . . Why look at me. See those intelligent eyes, ears, NOSE. . . . I'm totally lovable, can't you tell? . . . I've two telephones and of course thousands of rich admirers. . . . The world is at my feet and that is the way it should be. . . . Everybody says I am simply adorable. . . . And who am I to argue with the general consensus?

Who indeed. She walks through her beautifully decorated apartment—many of the walls have been sanded and plastered and painted by her—past the mantel filled with her bell collection. When asked what else she collects, Oleda Baker smiles her perfect smile. "Money," she responds, and laughs playfully.

Francey

"Oleda has her parents as her children because of money. And Francey is Oleda's number-one child," says the Reverend Petty. His wife, Francey, adds that materialistic values are "not the thing that makes us tick as they are with Oleda and Steve."

Not like Oleda in monetary desires, Francey, nine years younger than Oleda and born eleven years after Carmen, shares a number of characteristics with each sister.

Mrs. Freeman agrees: "Mary Frances is extremely intelligent—all my four children are. They're fast like their father. "My favorite child? Always your last one, you know. Your baby."

Everyone agrees Francey had the most lenient upbringing yet she remembers her childhood environment much as her siblings do: "Our home was never a nice Christian home. There was no love there. My parents didn't do anything to help anyone." She has created her own home differently, so it intertwines with her and her husband's religious involvement.

She speaks about being the wife of a minister: "I am rebellious toward the typical role. I don't dress the way I'm expected to dress." And she's too sensually attractive. "There are lots of expectations I don't fulfill." Husband Jim Petty disagrees: "She's been extremely successful in the role of minister's wife without trying to be; the thing that made her successful is not trying to be. She's *very* popular among the congregation. They admire her, look up to her, especially the young people. She's a leader among them; I think they identify with the independence, the glamour. . . . There's an inner beauty that I see." And there's an outer beauty everyone else notices. Tall—five feet, nine inches—with an incredibly tiny waist, shapely model-like hips and legs, high full breasts, and perfect posture, the long-haired striking woman could easily look cheap if she were not careful.

She is a meticulous, thorough individual. "Mary Francis is a little bossy to Jim," says Mrs. Freeman, "but he kind of likes it, you know." A parishioner comments, "I can't figure out who is taking care of whom in the Petty household." Big sister Oleda speaks of Francey's organization: "In life, she's a good chess player. And Jim is strong enough to live with this, and to admire this in her, the way she is so well organized. But if it interferes with what he wishes to do, he puts his foot down. He will say, 'Look, Francey, I'm not going to do this.' "

Mary Frances Freeman has been taking hold of her own life since she was a teenager. "I was a good student," she says, at North Miami High School and later at David Lipscomb College, in Nashville. "No, my parents didn't send me. Let's see. I think they contributed something, but I had worked summers. I had to

The glamorous Mrs. Petty gets ready for a church function. Says Oleda: "She looks no more like a minister's wife than I do."

lay off for a quarter" because of a lack of funds. Mr. and Mrs. Freeman were not enthusiastic about her seeking higher education, "although Daddy did want me out of the house; he was involved in his affairs. . . . I was the only one to go [to college] and that was because some of my peers were going. I had no encouragement or direction vocationally from my parents." She explains in her singsong southern voice that she played the piano since the age of eight and pursued it in college because "that was the obvious thing to major in" for someone who had never been exposed to any other career choices. Used to restrictions after growing up in the Freeman home, Francey found more of the same at the church-sponsored college. "I wanted to get away from that. I was so immature—I knew I didn't want to get married after seeing Oleda and Carmen. But I did want to get away from home."

But college did not excite her. She dropped out after a year and a half and moved in with Oleda—then a model in New York.

Francey was twenty-four when she met James Petty in New York City. He had become a minister of the Manhattan Church of Christ after graduating from New York University. Living with Oleda, Francey "had absolutely nothing in mind when I moved to New York. So I studied music [with a Juilliard teacher]. I was real good." She could have become a professional, she says.

When Francey was hired as secretary to a college president, she ended her musical training. "I *loved* performing, playing well. But I wasn't prepared to be involved in such a self-oriented profession. And I didn't want to travel." But she had no thoughts about what she did wish to do. "All of us sisters were so immature." Her husband adds, "They were well shielded."

While Francey was in New York, "Oleda kind of glued parts of my life back together. She's always been like a second mother to me." Francey began to mimic Oleda. "She helped me along with makeup, clothes, and helped me get a lot of self-confidence." Oleda encouraged Francey to become a model, but Francey says, "I could never picture myself in that field.

"I was more religious" than her siblings, "less warped" by the religious pressures at home. James Petty remembers, after meeting Francey when she attended his church, "We became very good friends and our friendship developed into a love relationship. It was not love at first sight." As their feelings deepened, Francey was offered a job with an advertising agency at the same time Jim decided to take a position in Philadelphia. Although they hadn't even kissed, Francey says, "I moved to Philadelphia to chase Jim." He left in July of 1966, Francey followed in February, and "we were engaged by April." Jim planned the total wedding—he had had, for many years, a side business of party planning and floral designing; it was a spectacular occasion.

"I was not a talkative person the first years of our marriage." Yet she threw her whole self into helping her husband, who she says "loves people. That was something new for me." A man who loved people? "No, *anybody* who loved people." She laughs, and adds, "Really and truly, my family was antisocial." She had to learn to be responsive to her husband, to others.

"I think that anything I want to do badly enough, I can do," and Francey decided she was going to fulfill the role of minister's wife to the best of her ability. But in her own way.

The couple moved to Montgomery, Alabama, for about four years, and, Jim says, "This was a real opportunity for both of us to do our thing, to experiment with a lot of programs." Together they wrote a book on the organizational aspects of church work. "And I set up the church office," says Francey. "I've done that in nearly every place we've gone. Then a secretary would be hired to keep it going."

Their two children were born in Alabama, Jamie, then Eve. The Pettys loved the church but hated Montgomery. "We were there in the late sixties when the redneck attitude was prevalent," states Jim in his Texas drawl, and they decided that he would take a ministry at Chicago's Northwest Church of Christ.

Francey remembers the years in various churches and comments on how fulfilling it was for her: "I realized there were some

better ways of living [than she had experienced within her home
during her childhood] and value to helping and being concerned
about other people. I found an avenue—through the church—to
do that. I think that's probably the thing that swayed me and still
keeps me religious. There's more to being on earth than being
selfish and grabbing everything for ourselves. We should help
other people as much as we can. Jim thinks it makes others happy,
and us happier." "Francey's really into that," says Jim. "That's
a big thing to her." Religion to her is action.

In Chicago, Jim recalls, "we did a lot of fostering"; they were
involved in numerous "benevolent acts," in Francey's words, as
they lived in an old house she loved and began renovating. Francey did the carpentry. And "I again organized the church office
and helped begin church programs. I was always assisting Jim in
his work." Jim explains that "most ministers' wives don't get into
the leadership roles like she does. In Chicago, we established a
preschool. She set it up." Francey canvassed the area to assess
need, inquired about state requirements.

Francey recalls that in the first years of her marriage: "I had
babies and I didn't want to do anything careerwise. I didn't want
to work or go to school while they were very young. When
Eve was three, she started school a half day [at the preschool]
and . . ."

Francey considered her future. Jim explains that Francey got
into the designing field because "that was my interest. That was
my second love. I kept talking about it. And she had a knack for
it. So I encouraged her to get training in it." She enrolled in the
Harrington Institute of Interior Design, a Chicago school, in a
program she thought essentially involved decorating. But she
found out differently. The interior and exterior design course
included drafting, preparing schematics, architectural render-
ings. She became knowledgeable about the building process.
Attending two nights a week, "I was working [on homework]
every day, and all the other nights." The following year she went
from eight until three P.M.; Jim watched Eve in the afternoons,

easily done because his office was at home. Francey observes, "I couldn't have done all I did without Jim's support, obviously. I think that's where a lot of women don't have the opportunity; a man doesn't want to do it, or can't." She continued her studies the following year until they decided to move to Fort Worth, where Jim became the minister of the huge Altamesa Church of Christ.

The move ended her formal training; the specialized Chicago school she attended had no equivalent in the Dallas-Fort Worth area. Jim and Francey considered her options and decided that if she designed a house for them incorporating her creative ideas, it could be used as a showplace for prospective clients for Francey's planned exterior design/interior decorating business.

Francey admits, "I knew nothing about building until we started our house. The reason I learned so much was that we had a lousy builder. And in the end, I finished the house. I was out

The Reverend Petty, his wife, and parishioners. Petty has told his spouse he is "flabbergasted at the down-grading husbands do to their wives . . . continually knocking them." And she adds, "I know I wouldn't have been able to do what I have if I didn't have Jim's support and encouragement, his telling me I can do it."

there with the subcontractors every day—working with them, learning and helping them at the same time."

Francey's house is spectacular. Tucked beneath the stairs sits her grand piano, and further to the right a game room. Mirrored surfaces abound. Fireplaces in the bedrooms, a planter banister, skylights, illuminated trees—an elegant, comfortable home. Oleda's paintings are scattered about; one, a picture of Francey and Jim's wedding in 1966, progresses to show the couple at future dates within their married life. Francey does not age at all, while Jim gets older and older. Tapestries hang on the walls. The children's playroom has a carpeted puppet stage.

As she steps out onto her deck Francey explains that her husband earns a top ministry salary; this allowed her to establish her business by building the modular, contemporary $175,000 home, the subject of an article in the Fort Worth *Star-Telegram,* "Minister's Home Not Traditional":

> . . . probably unlike any minister's house you've ever seen. . . . not traditional and . . . not conservative. . . . a razzle-dazzle kind of house that could upset people with preconceived notions of what a parsonage should be like, at least until they got to know the owners. Then they would realize that the Pettys are rather a unique couple, insofar as the preacher-and-his-wife image goes, and that individuality is reflected in their lifestyle. . . .
>
> Mrs. Petty drew up the plans according to what the couple agreed they wanted in a home: huge windows to let nature come inside and an airy, open feeling in a structure that would be "extremely functional, yet beautiful," she said.
>
> "Organization is my forte," she stated. "I try to find out what people want, put it together and present it to them."
>
> That statement could also describe her approach to house design. "I tried to make a sculpture out of it . . . a total unit both inside and out rather than having angles going every-which-way," she said. Mrs. Petty derived some inspiration by planning around the couple's collection of Orien-

Top: *The house that Francey built.* **Center:** *Stairwell, with piano beneath. Two steps lead to sunken gameroom, with a picture window overlooking the front lawn.* Bottom: *Dining room. Potted trees, eclectic antique furnishings abound.*

tal antiques and also relied on input from her husband. "He has that flair for the dramatic and exciting, leftover from his party-planning days."

. . . Mrs. Petty designed some custom-made built-ins and tables for the house. "Everything was placed and planned before we moved in," she said.

Mrs. Petty . . . thinks some church members were "surprised and shocked" by the house the minister's wife designed.

"I just do things I think I do well and stick to that, rather than try to play a certain role," said Mrs. Petty.

The house completed, the sociable Pettys began entertaining and showing their new home.

One acquaintance and church member invited to the Petty's house "was formulating plans to begin building houses on a part-time basis," remembers Francey, "but needed someone to help with house design, work with subcontractors, and do the supervising when he couldn't be around, also to work with clients on design and decorating aspects. He looked over our whole house and, just as he was leaving, decided to come back in and talk to me about our working together. Had I not been able to *show* what I could do in terms of designing and decorating a house, that relationship would not have been established. My husband really pushed the idea of designing and building a spectacular house, even though we could not afford it; it was a gamble of sorts."

For years, Francey supported and took part in her husband's career, and he was now reciprocating, encouraging her to utilize her talents, willing to put their money on the line. Francey likes and respects her spouse, and appreciates him. "I do think that Jim and I have a much more successful marriage than anybody we know. You don't see many happy marriages."

Most of Francey's work is done within her office at home, which has Eve's drawing over Francey's drafting table: "To Mom I love

Top: *Living area opening into dining room, in rear.* Bottom: *The Petty master suite.*

you." On her table lies a set of plans for a structure to be built on a nearby lake. Francey designs houses, inside and outside. "And I like doing boutiques, restaurants." Commercial design. Francey is not an architect; she has one finish her working drawings and get them approved.

Her profession as a designer and her first and continuing career—wife-of-the-minister, and mother—blend well together. But it is hard work. The Pettys entertain often and, she says, "It's increasingly difficult to handle yard work, housework, cooking, cleaning . . . Jim helps me with every one of those things, much more so than a lot of men do. But my business is growing!" She explains that she's a neat person, which makes her house look clean when it might not be—although to a guest, it appears spotless—and that her children "are old enough to clean their rooms every morning before they go to school. And they do it with hardly my reminding them." Her soft Texas-Florida accent rolls off her tongue and she smiles that beautiful Freeman smile.

Today her company, Francey Petty Designs, is involved with

Francey Petty at work on the site. Says a church-goer,
"How she gets so much done amazes me."

the building of several houses she was commissioned to design
and is drawing two more. She likes the total involvement, from
beginning to end, rather than "the usual interior decorating stuff.
There are a lot of interior decorators around who can do a good
job. But I supervise construction on the houses my partner and
I build." She is also negotiating a deal by which she alone will
construct a group of homes on speculation.

Francey took part in the decoration of Jim's church, located in
the Candleridge area of Fort Worth. The congregation numbers
over a thousand. Children running down the halls of the church
say, "Hi, Uncle Jim" to their minister, as he points to a room
explaining, "Francey's responsible for this," a parlor for brides
and funeral participants. She chose educational furnishings for
the church school's elementary grades, located within the massive church building which exists because, says Jim, "Texas is a
very strong area for the Church of Christ."

After being reared in a home revolving around the Church
of Christ, Francey continues a strong personal religious involvement along with her late-blooming career: "It's just a
matter of determination. Of course if you're married to someone who is hateful or a male chauvinist pig, or is trying to
hold you down, that's another problem. But if a woman is single or if she does have a man—but one who doesn't mind letting her do what she wants to do with her life—really, it's
only herself that's holding her back. They try to put the
blame on everybody else, society. I'm sure society has hurt us
in some areas. But I just think a person can do what she really wants to do."

She talks about the macramé canopy over the bed in her guest
bedroom, and how impressed people are, assuming she is a talented craftsperson when they see her handiwork. Actually she
dislikes sewing and handiwork, including macramé. "I hate it. But
because I didn't have the money, I had some guy show me some
knots. Then I started experimenting and I did it. Just by sheer
determination. I didn't know how to *draw a line* before I went to
school! I had never had a drafting course. Nothing! You talk

about feeling behind, and frustrated. And I was older than the kids as well."

"I think Oleda, Carmen, and I have a lot of determination to do something. And to try extra hard." Stephen Baker agrees: "They're all trying to prove themselves." He believes

"Francey doesn't cling to other women," says a friend. "She chooses to be an individual; she can do things alone. . . . And Jim doesn't do the talking for her— although before they came to Texas, Jim said to the elders here, 'Now look. My wife is an individual and you are not going to criticize her. She will do her thing, but she will never do anything to discredit the church. . . .' I think she took a few of the old-timers back a bit when she arrived. I don't know if they've gotten over it yet!"

the Freeman sisters developed their potential because it was an unfamiliar thing, not part of their childhood. "So as adults they are wide open to experience, and curious and enthusiastic about receiving these new experiences, and meeting new people."

Carmen, on her Carolina farm, queries: "Now do you know what makes a Late Bloomer?"

How Carmen Bailey Did It

1. After a difficult childhood, an unfortunate marriage, and mental illness, Carmen felt life was passing her by. She decided to start over.

2. "I'm not skilled for a specific job if I wanted one." One career not requiring formal education was farming.

3. Although her husband disapproved, she started a North Carolina farm.

4. Jack, with time, tried to bend and change enough to accept his wife's needs, but Carmen was unable to forget the unhappy years and separated from him.

5. Taking a particularly female approach, Carmen tended her livestock in a motherly manner. They thrived. And her creative approach to crop growing resulted in good yields. She and her two youngest children also fared well as they followed a diet almost exclusively of Bailey farm foods.

6. Although struggling financially, Carmen is—for the first time in her life—serene. She knows she's finally made the right choices.

How Oleda Baker Did It

1. Oleda married, had a baby, and became a model, finally traveling to New York City for this new career. She was essentially a Late-Blooming model, starting in her late twenties.

2. As her modeling days came to an end, she considered the possibilities; she tried handicrafts but found it unprofitable.

3. As a high-fashion model, she had been automatically accepted. She chose to take advantage of this, first by attempting to write a beauty book.

4. She was not discouraged by others. "You should never tell yourself no. After three or four say it, reconsider. But not until then. That's one of the biggest mistakes women make." But not Oleda.

5. As she faced her fortieth year, she saw the possibilities of mail-order cosmetics. And "I didn't say, 'It can't be done' or 'I don't know how' or 'It's too big for me to handle.' I just did it."

6. She utilized what she knew best—her modeling/beauty expertise. Models, when they end that phase of their lives, usually never enter another. But Oleda, instead of resting upon her past laurels, built her image into her own company, with spectacular success.

7. Her secretary describes Oleda as "very much today's woman." Oleda believes, "If I'm successful, it's due to more than my talent; it's my ability to choose the right people," such as her decision to enter into partnership with Schwartz, a mail-order wizard.

8. Oleda sees a direct line to late-blooming success. "There is no wavering," says the lady who combined her looks with an astute feel for the marketplace. Says a male associate, "She's a businessman, all the way."

How Francey Petty Did It

1. Francey married her minister-husband and, while her two children were babies, involved herself in church affairs.

2. Gaining administrative expertise and experience by organizing church offices and beginning a preschool, at the same time she enhanced her spouse's professional performance.

3. As her children entered school, Francey enrolled in a design curriculum. Jim helped her manage the unexpected long classroom and study hours by babysitting and sharing household chores.

4. The Pettys decided to build a home designed by Francey as an advertisement of sorts.

5. It worked. A contractor offered her a partnership.

6. Francey Petty Designs, still in its infancy stages, is rapidly expanding. The Reverend Petty's mental and physical support of his wife's new-found profession grows concurrently.

—— *Epilogue* ——

Can You Too Become
a Late Bloomer? Absolutely!

While the self-made male considers himself to be the architect of his accomplishments, the successful woman talks a great deal about luck. "It was fortunate I was in the right place at the right time." "If I hadn't met him, none of it would have ever happened." But after interviewing dozens of achieving females, I no longer believe in fate. For while every individual has opportunity cross her doorstep, there are a certain few who latch on to that chance and fly with it.

This is the ultimate lesson to be gleaned from this book. You and they share backgrounds, prebloom circumstances, levels of creativity, educational experience, age group, geographic location. Your story is here somewhere—at least the prebloom part—if perhaps spread among several biographical vignettes. And you and they have identical goals and hopes; if they, with their own particular limitations, could do it, so can you.

How? Step One has been made if you have recognized that "if only" is a useless phrase; it is time to act, forgetting past failures and considering future problems to be chances for thinking up creative solutions.

There are many how-to books and articles addressing themselves to you, which are helpful in raising your level of enthusiasm and drive. But note that the Late Bloomers' best instructional aide was a role model to relate to, coupled with their own personal commitment, for they, like you, are unique, with specific attributes and deficiencies. The how-to, ultimately, must come from within.

Do you now have the outlook with that maturity it takes to change your life's direction? Answer the following questions and consider each affirmative answer a building block to your future.

YES   NO   NOT SURE

1. Have you thought about your interests and experiences and clearly reached a decision, as Marty Harper did? Do *you* know what you want to do?

2. Are you willing to work extremely hard, with long hours, to reach your goal, the way June Eliel did and continues to do?

3. Have you accepted, as Gita Packer finally recognized, the notion that you must actively promote yourself?

4. Not one of the Late Bloomers found her new career through an agency. Have you faced the fact that, as a woman about to blossom, the energy needed to find your niche must finally come from you?

5. Do you realize, as Janice LaRouche did, that you must identify the individual who can help you to attain status, then systematically build a professional relationship with that person?

6. Elaine Bloom thoroughly analyzed her work-experience equivalents. Are you doing this?

7. When Dorothy White is interviewed for a job, she assumes she'll be hired and considers her perspective employer to be lucky to have her. Do you share such a positive personal assessment with Dot?

8. Are you unworried about your scanty education and absence of obvious marketable skills? And are you instead listing your attributes, areas of information?

9. If you want to attend school, do you plan to immerse yourself totally in a full-course plan, as

YES NO NOT SURE

Martha Radike did, rather than setting up a schedule that will take forever to complete?

10. Are you ready to utilize all your womanly qualities to succeed in a man's world, as Oleda Baker did? And did her experiences convince you that you, as a woman, are probably more adaptable, better organized, and more intuitive than your male competition?

11. Mary Clayburn recognizes that men of quality are not threatened by women of equality. Do you?

12. No matter what personal disasters Carmen Bailey has experienced, she believes in herself. What about you?

13. Mary Jane Jesse goes through life expecting wondrous things to happen. Are you, today, thinking optimistically?

14. Do you agree that a husband whose self-image hinges upon being the sole or superior wage earner and having a loftier job title is, at best, a shaky partner?

Let's consider for a moment husbands. Men. Marjorie Bell Chambers' spouse, a mature male, recognizes and applauds his wife's drive and potential. What about your man? Can he comprehend that your ambitions are ultimately for both of you, for the health of your relationship? Or is it hard for him to accept, and is he not terribly understanding, perhaps even jealous of your chance to begin anew? His attitudes should be sympathized with; he's recognizing that, as Janice LaRouche put it, "He will no longer be able to report the world to you"; you're going to be part of it.

I don't believe there is a husband alive who is not somewhat affected by his wife's late blooming. Society and his upbringing clash with his love and respect, and with the desires he has for his wife's happiness, and it takes a special man to be able to be supportive. It is not easy. Marty Harper's husband, David, shared such feelings with us, and it is therapeutic for men to know that it is natural and understandable to go through mental anguish. With soul searching, and as you begin to accomplish, he'll soon see a wife who is more sexually exciting, more full of life, enthusiasm, and sophistication.

As for you, your introspection is completed. It is time to act. Now. Two of the millionairesses I wrote of in my last book—twins who make bikinis—were asked for advice by a hopeful at-home entrepreneur. When should she rent a store? Begin production in earnest? Set up a functioning business? The millionairesses' simultaneous response: "Today! This afternoon!"

And expect success, miracles. But don't let the difficult steps trip you emotionally. Martha Radike says "people expect everything to be happy, happy, happy and perfect, perfect, perfect and life isn't like that; you have to learn to adjust, to accept certain things." One way to keep your spirits high—in addition to rereading a Late Bloomer profile or two for inspiration—is to plan your turnabout with another woman. Or with several. Together form a Late Bloomer League, assist one another, share thoughts, job leads, contacts. Work on résumés jointly. Practice imaginary job interviews. Mull over ideas. Lend support, encourage one another.

There is a new group of women who need to know it is possible to have a satisfying life after the children are gone, as the middle years arrive. Share your copy of *Late Bloomer* with them—with your daughter, your granddaughter, with younger females, high school and college graduates, who wonder if they can have babies (which might be the ultimate, meaningful role) in their twenties, then a career in their thirties, or later. Let Marilyn Stiefvater, Martha Radike, Francey Petty give them an affirmative answer, by example, and tips on how to establish a late-blooming occupation before having children, then resume it later.

And let me know how you are doing (c/o Harper & Row, Publishers, Inc., 10 East 53rd Street, New York, N.Y. 10022), and I'll try to pass along your comments and your experiences to others.

When I write *Late Bloomer II*, I want *you* in it.

A weed is no more than a flower in disguise.

—James Russell Lowell,
A Fable for Critics

About the Author

Lois Rich-McCoy was born in 1941 and grew up in Hollywood, Florida. She received her degrees from Goddard College (MS in science history) and has been a stockbroker, businesswoman, and research consultant. Articles by Mrs. McCoy have appeared in *Sail, Oceans, Harper's Bazaar, Family Weekly, Family Circle,* and *Fifty-Plus.* Her books include two on medical subjects and the widely acclaimed *Millionairess: Self-Made Women of America* (Harper & Row, 1979). She has visited over thirty cities, appearing on radio and television to discuss women and careers, and has spoken at Radcliffe, MIT, and the University of Miami.

Mrs. McCoy and her oceanographer husband, parents to four children, live in a Hudson River hamlet in New York State and spend summers in their Cape Cod homestead in Woods Hole.